Cambridge E

Elements in Publishing and Book Culture
edited by
Samantha Rayner
University College London
Leah Tether
University of Bristol

INNOVATIONS IN DIGITAL COMICS

A Popular Revolution

Francesca Benatti
The Open University

CAMBRIDGE
UNIVERSITY PRESS

CAMBRIDGE
UNIVERSITY PRESS

Shaftesbury Road, Cambridge CB2 8EA, United Kingdom

One Liberty Plaza, 20th Floor, New York, NY 10006, USA

477 Williamstown Road, Port Melbourne, VIC 3207, Australia

314–321, 3rd Floor, Plot 3, Splendor Forum, Jasola District Centre,
New Delhi – 110025, India

103 Penang Road, #05-06/07, Visioncrest Commercial, Singapore 238467

Cambridge University Press is part of Cambridge University Press & Assessment,
a department of the University of Cambridge.

We share the University's mission to contribute to society through the pursuit of
education, learning and research at the highest international levels of excellence.

www.cambridge.org
Information on this title: www.cambridge.org/9781009319966
DOI: 10.1017/9781009319942

First published 2024

A catalogue record for this publication is available from the British Library.

ISBN 978-1-009-31996-6 Paperback
ISSN 2514-8524 (online)
ISSN 2514-8516 (print)

Additional resources for this publication at www.cambridge.org/benatti_resources

Innovations in Digital Comics

A Popular Revolution

Elements in Publishing and Book Culture

DOI: 10.1017/9781009319942
First published online: June 2024

Francesca Benatti
The Open University

Author for correspondence: Francesca Benatti, francesca.benatti@open.ac.uk

ABSTRACT: The success of popular webcomics (comics produced and read entirely digitally) is the greatest revolution in the comics medium of the last two decades. Webcomics exploit a socio-technical convergence between digital platforms and participatory cultures, enabling global authors to work together with global audiences to transcend established print comics structures. After defining digital comics, webcomics and webtoons, this Element presents a case study of Korean platform WEBTOON, which achieved 100 billion global page views in 2019. The study analyses data from their website, including views, subscriptions and likes, to quantify and assess whether WEBTOON's commercial and critical success is connected to its inclusion of a wider range of genres and of a more diverse author base than mainstream English-language print comics. In so doing, it performs the first Book Historical study of webcomics and webtoons. This title is also available as Open Access on Cambridge Core.

KEYWORDS: comics, webcomics, publishing, webtoons, gender

ISBNs: 9781009319966 (PB), 9781009319942 (OC)
ISSNs: 2514-8524 (online), 2514-8516 (print)

Contents

Additional resources for this publication at
www.cambridge.org/benatti_resources

Disclaimer

[DISCLAIMER] – Data reflects WEBTOON's US platform only, and was gathered prior to a 2023 Terms of Service update that now prohibits data scraping. The data presented was not provided or validated by WEBTOON, and may vary from current platform usage.

1 From Digital Comics to Webcomics to Webtoons

1.1 Introduction

In the third decade of the twenty-first century, comics have gained an unprecedented amount of visibility, with comics-derived content dominating multiple media from film to television to videogames. No longer perceived as the purview of insular fandoms, comics have emerged as a fundamental pillar of globalised popular culture. The fortune of comics within transmedia spaces has reflected positively on their original print medium, at least within the traditional English-language industry based in the United States. The turmoil of the 2020–2021 Covid pandemic served as a further catalyst to develop new strategies and channels to diversify its distribution and sales infrastructures, leading to unprecedented sales in 2020 and 2021 (Griepp 2022).

Some of the most profound innovations in comics to emerge in the past two decades lie not within print, however, but in the emergence and consolidation of webcomics, which are an evolving medium that can be defined as 'graphic sequential narratives that are created, published, and read on-line' (Priego Ramirez 2011 p. 267). The majority of comics published in the twenty-first century are to an extent digital, as they are produced, distributed and consumed in ways that are 'mediated through a computer' (Resha 2020 p. 70). However, certain comics embrace the digital in every phase of their lifecycles and exist solely in non-material, digital formats. Defined widely as digital comics, webcomics and webtoons, webcomics represent an increasingly significant area for the readers and creators of comics, but remain still undertheorised from a scholarly point of view (Misemer 2021 p. 218). The difference between digital comics and webcomics is, for example, still unclearly defined. Similarly, the very flexibility of webcomics, which are freed from the limitations of print technologies and of the printed page, make a formal definition challenging. Being often produced by independent creators without a publisher's oversight, webcomics have little or no limits in terms of subject matter. This lack of barriers also renders them an ideal platform for creators from marginalised communities to address their audience directly (Robbins 2013 p. 168).

Because of the 'close association between the development of digital technology and the medium of webcomics' (Misemer 2021 p. 220), webcomics need to be studied within the historical and technological context of their production and reception. Within the last 30 years, the development and adoption of internet technologies have enabled webcomics to establish themselves as a ground for experimentation and exploration. The widespread adoption of ubiquitous mobile computing through smartphones and the diffusion of social media platforms have created new possibilities for webcomics in format, distribution and remuneration, which have converged in South Korea to give rise to a new and underexplored webcomics genre, the webtoon.

Inspired by the approaches of pioneering historians of the books such as Robert Darnton (Darnton 1982), Roger Chartier (Chartier 1995) and William St Clair (St Clair 2004), of historians of the digital book such as Padmini Ray Murray, Claire Squires (Ray Murray and Squires 2013), R. Lyle Skains (Skains 2019) and Melanie Ramdarshan-Bold (Ramdarshan Bold 2018), and by webcomics scholars such as Leah Misemer (Misemer 2019a, 2021) and Adrienne Resha (Resha 2020), this Element will assess the communication circuits of webcomics and webtoons and ask whether the growing success of the medium can be related to the level of participation it affords to female and nonbinary authors, and to the wider range of genres it includes. It will do so by comparing webtoon authorship and publishing practices with those of more mature formats such as US superhero comics and by plotting female and nonbinary participation in those circuits against those of webtoons. It will quantify the authorship and readership of what is currently the largest webtoon publisher, the English-language version of the South Korean platform (Naver) WEBTOON, which achieved 100 billion global page views in 2019 (MacDonald 2020a). It will analyse the presence of female and nonbinary authors in a sample composed of the 80 most read WEBTOON comics, classifying them also by their genre. Finally, it will assess whether the opportunities and remuneration offered by WEBTOON enable more diverse comics creators to obtain recognition, or whether the mechanisms of the digital 'attention economy' (Goldhaber 1997) and of the 'platformisation' of cultural production (Helmond 2015 p. 1) confine them to gruelling and uncertain employment at the mercy of readers and new digital taskmasters.

Authors have always depended on capturing the favour of the public, as acknowledged by David Garrick in 1747, when he stated that ' . . . we that please to live, must live to please' (Johnson and Garrick 1763). Garrick's speech, as reported by Samuel Johnson, implies the complete dependence of the author upon the favour of the public, who will not purchase what it does not like. In the current attention economy, however, the challenge for authors is no longer how to make their work public, but how to get noticed by an ever-busier global audience. A platform such as WEBTOON can help authors with both: it takes care of the software systems that enable publishing, counts page views and audience engagement, negotiates advertisement deals, and for those few authors able to get contracted, it acts as a publisher, providing a form of regular income, as well as editorial assistance and promotion. It does so in exchange for a share of the profits and for a significant level of control on the creators' freedom of expression, from content limitation and genre classification, to a more widespread 'platformisation' of creative labour (Duffy et al. 2019; Kim and Yu 2019). This Element assesses whether publication on WEBTOON represents a worthwhile trade-off for authors, especially if female or nonbinary, or whether it constitutes a backward step compared to the creative freedom of independent webcomics.

To understand these questions, the operations of WEBTOON must first be positioned within the context of webcomics and their development over the past 30 years.

1.2 Defining Digital Comics, Webcomics and Webtoons

The terms digital comics, webcomics and webtoons refer to contiguous or overlapping fields which must be clarified before developing the rest of this study.

1.2.1 Digital Comics

As stated by Resha, almost all comics published in the twenty-first century are to a certain extent digital, as they are produced, distributed and consumed in ways that are 'mediated through a computer' (Resha 2020

p. 70). For example, numerous phases of the creation of comics, such as colouring and lettering, are nowadays carried out through digital drawing devices and tools. These include, for example, graphic tablets manufactured by, among others, Wacom, Microsoft, Apple and Samsung, and specialised drawing apps such as Clip Studio Paint. Developing Resha's arguments, this study defines digital comics as comprising all comics that can be read through digital devices such as computers, e-readers or smartphones.

This broad definition is based primarily on the 'Medium' employed for reading rather than the 'Content' it carries, as defined in the READ-IT ontology of the reading experience (Antonini et al. 2019 p. 7). As such, it does not distinguish between comics originally created for print and those that have been planned as being solely digital. These can be theorised instead with reference to the cognate field of electronic literature, which hinges around the distinction between digitised works and born-digital works (Hayles 2008 p. 3). In electronic literature, digitised works are derived from physical antecedents, such as books or artworks, while born-digital works have no material artefact that constitutes their 'original' status. By applying the same logic to comics, digital comics can therefore be defined as including both *digitised* comics, which are digital 'reproductions' (Resha 2020 p. 70) of comics previously released in print, and *born-digital* comics, which are created, published and read in the first or only instance through digital media.

Examples of digitised comics include those available from the online portals of major publishers such as DC Universe Infinite and Marvel Unlimited, which reproduce for online reading current and past issues of the publishers' respective catalogues. These may include additional features such as animations or 3D images (Resha 2020 p. 71), but they remain fundamentally copies or, more precisely, versions of comics originally conceived for print. Digitised comics usually transpose on the screen formats that originate from print, such as the 6.63 by 10.24 inches (16.84 by 26.01 cm) page of US print comics. Given the landscape orientation of computer screens, this migration from one medium to another is not trivial and may require adaptations or trade-offs. For example, the digitised comics store ComiXology, founded in 2007, has developed a software called 'Guided View' that allows readers to navigate a comic by zooming in on one single panel at a time (Priego and Wilkins 2018 p. 9). While providing a solution for viewing comics pages on small screens, the use of panel-by-panel navigation tools has been claimed to be responsible for a 'compromised reading experience' with regard to reader immersion and comprehension (Hou et al. 2017 p. 92). Digitised comics are therefore constrained by the processes necessary to adapt one original medium (print) into another (digital) (Batinić 2022a p. 86).

1.2.2 Webcomics

Webcomics are a born-digital comics format that still lacks a univocal definition, though several scholars have identified specific salient aspects. Ernesto Priego identifies webcomics as comics 'that are created, published, and read on-line' (Priego Ramirez 2011 p. 267). Josip Batinić underlines their structural inclusion of elements of internet web pages (Batinić 2022b p. 350). Sean Kleefeld bases his definition on authorial intent, deeming a digital comic to be a webcomic if the author meant it to be read on the web in the first place. He also underlines the independence of webcomics from specific, proprietary software that mediates the reader's viewing experience (Kleefeld 2020 pp. 2–4). Leah Misemer distinguishes webcomics, which are 'digital native', from digital comics, which are printed comics reproduced in digital form, and acknowledges above all their diversity and flexibility (Misemer 2021 p. 218). This study draws from the work of these scholars to define webcomics as born-digital comics that are intended and designed by their authors to be read on digital screens such as computers, tablets or smartphones, and that are circulated through internet networks. As born-digital artefacts, webcomics are digital not solely in specific phases of their lifecycles but at all times throughout them, with digital representing their 'original' format. Webcomics are therefore a subset of digital comics.

Webcomics as a novel publishing format emerged when certain technological inventions, such as digital drawing devices and web protocols, were adopted and appropriated by creators and readers. These manifold agents transformed such inventions into a set of innovations to comics formats and contents (Baudry 2018 p. 4), which should always be studied within their specific social and historical contexts (Misemer 2019a p. 2). For example, in the days of the early internet, website creation required coding skills that only a few possessed, restricting the potential pool of webcomics creators (Misemer 2021 p. 220). Similarly, the limited speed of the early internet drove authors towards short-format comics that could be downloaded on dial-up connections (Campbell 2006 p. 19). As faster broadband connections expanded their reach and affordability, longer-form webcomics became a viable proposition. The web thus drastically reduced printing and distribution costs, historically one of the main obstacles to independent comics (Fenty et al. 2004 p. 5) and placed comics published on websites solely under the creators' control, without gatekeepers or intermediaries (Misemer 2021 p. 218), though the last statement will be qualified in later sections.

Since the early studies on webcomics, scholars have identified formal flexibility as one of the defining traits of webcomics, which can transcend the limitations of the printed page into an 'infinite canvas' (McCloud 2000 p. 200). Other scholars have maintained that webcomics are continuing and extending the disruptive revolutions of underground comics, permitting experimentation in both form and content (Fenty et al. 2004 sec. 22). More recent studies have qualified this seemingly unlimited potential with a recognition of the skeuomorphism of most webcomics (Martin 2017; Resha 2020 p. 71). Firstly, scholars have observed that, despite experimental interfaces such as Daniel Goodbrey's multi-cursal works (Goodbrey n.d.), the majority of webcomics still recognisably 'look like' comics and maintain elements that are 'specific to ... [comics'] media identity' such as 'sequentiality, speech bubbles' (Baudry 2018 p. 1) (McCloud 1994 p. 66). Webcomics continue to an extent to resemble the printed comics page or the three- or four-panel newspaper strip. Moreover, it can be argued that even while existing only on digital screens, most webcomics retain the grid-like 'enframing' devices of the print page (Priego and Wilkins 2018 p. 17). Additionally, the digital graphics tools that are opening webcomics authorship to non-programmers contribute to their gravitation towards 'a limited number of recurrent formats' and structures (Rageul 2018 p. 8) through their intermediation as cultural software (Manovich 2013 p. 20).

1.2.3 Webtoons

Given the dependencies identified by Misemer between the mode (digital technology) and the medium of webcomics, (Misemer 2019a p. 2), it is not surprising that two of the most decisive technological changes of the last two decades are having an impact on webcomics: the diffusion of mobile internet-capable devices such as smartphones and the rise of social media platforms. Webtoons (a portmanteau of web and cartoons) can be seen as a variety of the webcomics medium created to respond to the technological mode of mobile devices. They are a subset of webcomics with distinctive formal characteristics that make them particularly suitable for consumption and distribution on mobile devices. To achieve this end, webtoons have distanced themselves further from the print paradigms that still characterise most webcomics (see Section 1.2.3). Arguably, webtoons provide the first true remediation of the comics medium in a digital context, in the original sense of a 'critique and refashion' of prior analogue media (Bolter and Grusin 1996 p. 343). They do so by abandoning the grid 'enframing devices' of print and adopting instead a continuous vertical scroll that privileges the panel as 'the base unit of the comics system' (Groensteen 2007 p. 35). This remediation negates the derivative structures of print publication such as openings, which are often employed in print comics to display panels that stretch beyond the individual page, and page turnings, which can be used to underline dramatic plot points. Instead of gutters, webtoon panels are separated by variable amounts of screen space, which can be left blank or filled with graphics and colours. The variable distance between panels can also be employed to 'express the duration of time' (Cho 2016), since wider space between panels requires more time spent scrolling before reading the following chunk of content. Lettering practices too are altered by the move to mobile devices, with the small screen sizes requiring proportionally larger speech balloons and font sizes than print publications and most webcomics. Brazilian comics scholar and practitioner Alexandra Presser has highlighted these and other fundamental design differences between vertical-scroll webtoons and print comics in a series of research articles and practical guides (Presser 2019; Presser et al. 2021). The vertical scrolling webtoon format is proving so effective on mobile devices that even established US print publishers such as DC and Marvel are experimenting with it, the former by publishing a number of series on WEBTOON Originals (see Section 3), the latter by including vertical scrolling 'infinity comics' in its mobile Marvel Unlimited app. The most notable webtoons, however, remain at the moment those published on Korean platforms, such as Naver WEBTOON, Kakao/Daum, Lezhin and others.

The impact on webcomics of the second change mentioned above, the rise and diffusion of social media, will be examined in more detail in Sections 1.4 and 2.3.

1.3 Webcomics in the US: Historical Context

As shown above, webcomics can be considered 'the comics vanguard' in their innovations of the comics medium within constantly shifting digital technologies (Misemer 2021 p. 221). The communications circuit of webcomics has been little studied so far, at least from a history of the book point of view. Where critical attention has been given to the comics medium, it has concentrated on the more established print genres of serialised magazine comics, such as, for example, superhero comics, or on graphic novels, a term now applied to all comics published in book format. This relative slighting of webcomics was understandable while webcomics and the internet itself were a novelty of uncertain future, but they have now been in existence for almost 40 years, with a history that is intertwined with the development of the World Wide Web and of its socio-technical evolution.

In order to evaluate the innovations introduced by webcomics, it is first necessary to locate them within the established circuits of print comics and to trace a brief history of their development. Both the communication circuit of print comics and that of webcomics can be plotted against Robert Darnton's print 'communications circuit' (Darnton 1982 p. 67), for example, by comparing the established production process of US superhero comics (Benatti 2019). The 'direct sales' or 'direct market' system that held sway over English-language comics publishing for 50 years grants greater authority to certain agents within the circuit. While in Darnton's model the author is the dominant force, in the US comics circuit, the most significant influence resides with the publishers, who exercise it through the activity of editors and sub-editors. This accumulation of power in the hands of the publishers depends largely upon their hold on the 'economic rights' (Gordon 2013 p. 223) of the most prominent US comics content, superhero characters, which resides with them and not with their creators (Sabin 1993

p. 32). A lack of competition was evident until recently in other key areas of the print comics circuit. Periodical comics, known as 'pamphlets' or 'floppies', are available exclusively through specialist comics stores. These fulfil the role of Darnton's 'Booksellers' and are in turn served by a limited number of distribution companies, which provide them with comics on a mostly non-returnable basis. Chief amongst them is still Diamond Comics, which, until 2020, had a virtual monopoly on the supply of periodical comics. The upheavals of the Covid-19 pandemic, which included a complete shutdown of Diamond's operations for a number of weeks in 2020 (MacDonald 2020b), prompted a reevaluation of this control. For example, DC Comics decided to shift its periodicals distribution to a new company, Lunar Distribution, in June 2020 (McMillan 2020), while Marvel opted in 2021 to work with Penguin Random House (MacDonald 2021), where it was later joined by Dark Horse and IDW (MacDonald 2022b). Once periodical comics have been collected into book format 'graphic novels', they can also be sold through book channels, such as physical and online bookstores, where more varied distribution and sales options exist. Several smaller publishers such as Boom! Studios, Oni Press and TKO, for example, employ book trade distributors such as Simon & Schuster to reach the bookstore market (MacDonald 2022b). Comic stores, however, remain the only outlet for purchasers of monthly issues of ongoing periodical comics.

Models are always prone to the risk of oversimplification, and the one delineated above is no exception. It has been argued that already from the 2010s, the US comic books industry has fragmented into 'range of different models in different formats and channels addressing different audiences' and can no longer be equated solely with comics publishing (Woo 2018 p. 38). Webcomics have played a decisive role in this diversification from the time they emerged with the growth of personal computers and of the World Wide Web. The first digital comics, such as Joe Ekaitis' *T.H.E. Fox* (1986–1998) and Hans Bjordahl's *Where the Buffalo Roam* (1987–1995) indeed preceded the development of the WWW, with the first webcomics in the sense of Priego's definition (see Section 1.1) considered to be Stafford Huyler's *NetBoy* and David Farley's *Doctor Fun*, both begun in 1993 (Kleefeld 2020 pp. 20–1). In this initial phase, webcomics authors relied on self-hosted websites, which they often designed and maintained on their own. As mentioned in Section 1.2.2, the high technological bar required for computer graphics and website creation limited webcomics publication, for a while, to creators who were skilled in web programming, who also often chose technology or videogames as subject matter (Kleefeld 2020 pp. 22–6), as can be seen, for example, in several successful webcomics from the 1990s, such as Scott Kurtz's *PvP* and Mike Krahulik and Jerry Holkins's *Penny Arcade*, both started in 1998 and are still ongoing.

A determining trait of all early webcomics, which shaped the medium into the future, was their being offered to readers' consumption without the need for any payment. This free and ubiquitous availability contributed to the dissemination of webcomics to wide global audiences. At the same time, it established a set of expectations that complicated future sustainability in terms of both providing a living for creators and covering infrastructural costs. In this initial phase, webcomics authors relied on self-hosted websites, which they often designed and maintained on their own. While the cost of web hosting reduced over time as the internet gained pervasiveness, it nonetheless still entailed expenditure and responsibilities for creators, which, in print circuits, would be delegated to publishers.

With the rise of online content platforms such as blogs, webcomics creators were able to rely on these standardised web technologies to aid them in the creation of their websites, for example, through plugins such as ComicPress for the WordPress content management system. These models lessened the burden of website design and led to the gradual establishment of common formats and structures (Rageul 2018 p. 8) in webcomics sites, such as separate pages for current issues and archives pages (Kleefeld 2020 p. 31).

Due to the technological restrictions discussed above (see Section 1.2.2), early webcomics tended to privilege short episodic strips, usually composed of a small number of panels. Thematically these early comics often focused on humorous content and were reminiscent in their structure of newspaper comic strips, which they also resembled in their frequent periodicity of publication (often daily or weekly) (Allen 2014 p. 152; Garrity 2011). These shorter comics could be produced by a single author who created both words and artwork, in contrast with US print comics, which are usually 'collectively produced' (Mag Uidhir 2012 p. 47) as part of 'an industrial form of art' (Manouach 2019 p. 5). Many webcomics authors turned these limitations to their advantage, employing the freedom of creating and publishing their own content to explore controversial or niche topics that would have struggled to find acceptance through mainstream print channels (Fenty et al. 2004 p. 2).

The absence of publishers meant that most readers tended to discover early webcomics through word-of-mouth recommendations or fan-created 'aggregators such as Comic Rocket and Piperka' (Zhdanova 2021). Creators also organised to promote each other's works, for example, through reciprocal guest comics, where two or more authors would create episodes in another author's webcomic (Misemer 2019a p. 6) or through authors' collectives such as Hiveworks. These collectives offered creators the chance to achieve greater visibility and to establish a space where reader communities could coalesce into 'correspondence zones' where readers and authors could enter into a collaborative dialogue (Misemer 2019b p. 10) that became fundamental for the webcomics communications circuit (see Section 1.4).

While the freedom to experiment with content and format could empower webcomics creators, securing an income through them proved a challenge. To address it, webcomics creators experimented with aggregation portals that provided access through a subscription model. The most successful was Modern Tales, created in 2001 by author and tech entrepreneur Joey Manley. Modern Tales charged readers a monthly fee in exchange for access to a selection of original webcomics such as Shaenon K. Garrity's *Narbonic*, James Kochalka's *American Elf* and Lea Hernandez's *Rumble Girls*. Hernandez and Manley went on to launch a subscription portal focused on female authors, Girlamatic. As well as including already established authors such as Rachel Hartman and Hernandez, Girlamatic provided the first publishing opportunity for female comics authors such as Raina Telgemeier, C. Spike Trotman, Svetlana Chmakova and Hope Larson, who later secured contracts with print publishers. Despite these promising beginnings, 'the money was never good' (Garrity 2013). The aggregation and subscription model pioneered by Modern Tales and Girlamatic never succeeded in providing a living wage to its featured comics creators, eventually closing down in 2013. Narratives of creative freedom and authorial autonomy in early webcomics must thus be balanced against the difficulties of establishing viable economic models that could enable authors to sustain an enduring career as webcomics creators alone (Misemer 2021 p. 221).

As mentioned above, the rise of social media platforms such as Facebook, Tumblr, Twitter and Instagram in the 2010s triggered significant changes in webcomics (Misemer 2019a). Numerous creators switched to these as the main hosting site or at least the main promotional channel for their webcomics. While the ubiquity of social media enabled rapid distribution, creators that relied on them often faced struggles with their restrictions in terms of allowed content and suitability for long-form comics. Artist-focused platforms such as DeviantArt (www.deviantart.com), founded in 2000 to enable artists to share visual content, provided for a while a viable alternative for comics creators wanting to experiment with controversial content, including sexually explicit comics such as Stjepan Šejić's *Sunstone* (Šejić 2018). Though structured to privilege the upload of standalone rather than sequential images, comics hosted on DeviantArt could act as a portfolio for aspiring creators. The popularity of *Sunstone* on DeviantArt, for example, persuaded Matt Hawkins, CEO of US publisher Top Cow Comics, an imprint of Image Comics, to publish the series in print, where it established itself as its bestselling graphic novel. Hawkins has noted in particular its appeal to an unprecedented audience, such as 'women in their mid-30s', who had never before been prominent among Top Cow customers (Hawkins et al. 2018 p. 123). The publisher proceeded to capitalise on this unexpected success by expanding the publication of *Sunstone*, which has now reached its seventh volume, and by producing further comics set in the same story world, such as Linda Šejić's *Blood Stain* (2016–ongoing) and her collaboration with Hawkins, Jenni Cheung and Yishan Li, *Swing* (2018–2022). Stjepan and Linda Šejić are an example of 'hybrid authors' (Skains 2019 p. 21) who have been able to use free digital content, such as webcomics, to propel or enhance a career in print. It must, however, be noted that their remarkable success is matched by only a minority of webcomics authors. Most webcomics creators fail to establish a network of similar proportions and gravitate instead towards the growing communities of digitally based, self-employed creatives threading multifarious paths in search of financial sustainability.

During the 2000s, perhaps the most important of such income streams was the hosting of online advertisements on comics websites (Allen 2014 p. 60). Crucial in this process was the establishment of programmes from search engines such as Google AdSense (www.google.com/intl/en_uk/ adsense/start/). While this model was widespread, webcomics sites hosted online advertisements, usually placed on the margins of the page, such as being positioned as a banner above or below the main creative content. Their hosting paid creators a fee based on the number of ad impressions (how many times an ad is downloaded to a device), clickthrough rates (the number of readers who proceed to click on the advertisements) and conversions (actions performed on the advertiser's website as a result of following the link). For comics with high readership figures, the revenue from advertisements could provide a useful baseline income. The potential of this revenue stream led comics creator Ryan North to launch a webcomics-specific online advertising service, Project Wonderful, in 2006, which until its closure enabled creators to publish unobtrusive, targeted ads on their comics' website, something North hoped could benefit both creators and publishers. This approach was challenged from the mid-2010s by the development of adblocker software, which prevented ads from being loaded into users' computers, thus reducing advertising income to negligible figures even for successful comics. Webcomics creator Rich Burlew, for example, remarked that for his comic *Order of the Stick* (discussed in greater detail in this section) 'advertising revenue dropped off to zero a year or so ago' (2020). These developments led to the demise of Project Wonderful in 2018.

Another income stream embraced early on by webcomics creators was merchandising sales, especially in the shape of t-shirts and other objects derived from the comic (Allen 2014 p. 56). Specialised companies, such as TopatoCo, arose to enable the production and distribution of these objects and continue trading to this day (https://topatoco.com/). These forms of monetisation proved popular in the late 2000s and early 2010s, but by the middle of the decade they too had witnessed a decline, as visible, for example, through the income figures posted yearly by webcomic creators such as Dorothy Gambrell, author of *Cat and Girl*, between 2010 and 2016 (see Gambrell 2017) and Ryan Estrada (see Davis 2012). Another income stream, the sale of original comics artwork, is often precluded to webcomics creators by their reliance on digital processes. As intrinsically born-digital works, the main components of a webcomic, such as script, line artwork, colours, and balloons, are produced through digital drawing and writing tools only, without a material antecedent. There is therefore no 'original' drawing that can be sold to dedicated readers and collectors. The only exception are artworks traded with readers who participate in the burgeoning circuit of comics conventions, where webcomics authors are making increasingly frequent appearances.

From the 2010s, webcomic creators began to place a greater reliance on direct financing from small but dedicated reader communities. Two of the most successful strategies to date include 'subscription-based' and 'rewards-based' crowdfunding (Dowthwaite 2017 pp. 61–2). With subscription micropayments, readers contribute small amounts directly to the author, usually on an ongoing basis. The chief platforms for subscriptions are Patreon, founded in 2013, and Substack, created in 2017. Creators usually offer several subscription tiers, with additional rewards such as early access and additional content, for example, sexually explicit 'not safe for work' (NSFW) materials, as an enticement to higher contributions. The main goal of subscription remains the generation of a reliable baseline income for the creator rather than the provision of a specific product. This is instead the remit of rewards-based crowdfunding platforms such as Kickstarter, which are principally employed to finance the creation of tangible objects, such as volumes collecting a sequence of issues in print, or specific items of merchandise. The advantage for authors of employing platforms like Kickstarter lies in their ability to verify the extent of their financial backing before embarking on the onerous processes of publishing and distribution. If a collected volume does not reach its funding target, it is not printed, and all money is returned to the prospective backers. The crowdfunding campaign that above all demonstrated the viability of this income stream for webcomics was conducted in 2012 by Rich Burlew, creator since 2004 of the webcomic *Order of the Stick*, which focuses on the apparently niche world of fantasy roleplaying games (www.giantitp.com/comics/oots.html).

Burlew was able to raise $1.2 million to republish in print the content of his free webcomic, breaking previous records for the amount raised by creative projects and showing other creators that 'the whole "free content" model' (Cavna 2012) had significant potential. The success of Burlew's campaign also brought into sharper relief to the mainstream media the ability of webcomics to configure a communications circuit that is alternative to that of print comics. The next section will discuss how this circuit bears numerous resemblances to the digital publishing communications circuit highlighted by Padmini Ray Murray and Clare Squires (Ray Murray and Squires 2013) and to the evolution of digital authorship outlined by Skains (Skains 2019).

1.4 The Webcomics Communication Circuit

In the webcomics communication circuit, authors begin by publishing their content for free on the internet, usually through self-hosted websites. Webcomics authors enable and indeed solicit reader participation in processes such as editing, distribution, promotion and financing in a complex 'reshaping of roles' that has been described for books by Ray Murray and Squires (2013 pp. 16–8) and for comics by Misemer (Misemer 2019b p. 10). Webcomics instantiate this model by, on the one hand, fragmenting the various phases of Darnton's circuit, as there is no centralized oversight by any organisation. On the other hand, webcomics rely on a 'blending of creation and experience' for the readers, who combine reading with engagement and reflection through, for example, social media activity, as articulated by Antonini, Brooker and Benatti (Antonini et al. 2020 p. 297). The success of webcomics depends in part on the ability of authors to involve a base of dedicated and committed readers, who are willing to support the author in a relationship that sits between quasi-patronage and co-authorship. Webcomics readers cannot purchase physical artefacts with the same ease as print comics readers, but they can lend their support through other behaviours, such as regular reading, engagement through a variety of social media, and financial provision. This involvement with different phases of authorial production builds upon the foundational role that comics reading occupies in the creation of identities among their public, as discussed by Cedeira Serantes (2019 p. 83). This strategy of continuous, two-way reader involvement is the cornerstone of the webcomics communications circuit and makes full use of their affordances.

First among them is the combination of reader involvement with serialisation, enabling frequent publication that receives almost immediate feedback from readers, for example, through comments or social media activities. Comics can be a serial medium irrespective of whether they are printed or digital. They differ from other serial media, such as television, by usually including an element of work-in-progress. A television serial is generally released in seasons composed of multiple episodes, whose filming and production are fully completed before their release to the public. In a print periodical comic, readers encounter the work at fixed intervals, usually monthly. Each instalment of a print comic has been fully finished before its release to the public, though the entire larger series or story arc it forms part of may not be completed before the first instalment is released. The publishing cycles of webcomics are even more accelerated. Shorter publication schedules, such as on a 'daily or weekly' (Antonini et al. 2020 p. 289) basis, are preferred, through forms of continuous, rapid serialisation. Once certain milestones have been reached, such as a given number of pages or the conclusion of a story arc, the work-in-progress may be collected in formats such as digital or printed volumes. This frequent publishing schedule contributes to the heavy involvement of webcomics creators in the formation of parasocial relationships, imagined relationships that consumers have with the producers of content (Horton and Wohl 1956). In the case of webcomics, these relationships are usually expressed through the creators' social media presence, where maintenance of an online persona becomes an expectation for readers and a requirement for authors. This shift to a more creator-centric approach therefore leverages the desire for continuous connection and interaction between readers and creators, which is also evident in other sections of the 'digital literary sphere' (Murray 2015 pp. 322–3) and in the digital creative economy more broadly.

The second significant affordance for webcomics readers is their ability to inscribe their own interpretations on the very same page that contains the author's utterances (Liu 2013). Avenues for these responses are, for example, comments in the margin of the comics page or even upon the page itself (such as in Japanese *tsukkomi*). In the resulting multiplicity of voices, the pronouncements from the readers surpass those by the author in quantity, if not in authority, and contribute to the creation of a communications circuit that is based on a decentralised, distributed and hypertextual model, rather than a hierarchical one. Through the digital webcomics circuit, readers take therefore on the feedback role traditionally ascribed to critics. They acquire the ability to target their observations with unprecedented granularity and rapidity, making their influence felt on the author before a webcomic series is even completed.

The third affordance of webcomics is their capacity to decentralise those editorial and financial activities that, in a print circuit, would fall under the remit of the publisher. As independent publications, self-published webcomics are not overseen by professional editors but are often supported by 'self-organised volunteers or para-professional groups' who coagulate from the reading public (Antonini et al. 2020 p. 291). Readers' roles range from the formal or informal feedback mentioned above, to proofreading, translation into other languages and word-of-mouth marketing through social media. Subscription-based and reward-based crowdfunding projects provide readers with the ability to spread the onus of supporting their favourite authors across a wider community. This condition resembles the subscription publishing models employed by eighteenth- and nineteenth-century authors and publishers (Findlay 2010), though, in the digital age, it is characterised by faster turnaround times and a more globalised subscriber base. To succeed at crowdfunding, authors need to rely on a combination of factors including their social media skills, their status or recognition and their project's artistic style, which can entice and attract supporters (Pereira de Carvalho 2016 p. 255). Even in the more level playing field of webcomics, novice authors experience greater difficulties than more established ones, who already possess 'cultural capital' and recognition (Pereira de Carvalho 2016 p. 261).

Furthermore, the use of digital technologies for the creation, distribution and fruition of webcomics introduces challenges to their long-term access and preservation. With no material equivalent to fall back on, webcomics are ephemeral and at an even greater risk of disappearance than the already fragile periodical comics. This situation is again not a complete novelty.

Nineteenth-century periodicals, which were arguably the first mass media, were similarly perceived as 'ephemeral' commodities (Beetham 1990 p. 19) not meant for preservation but for short-term perusal only. It was chiefly by being published in book format that the novels and essays they contained managed to reach a form of stability across time, to the extent that the serial origin of numerous Victorian works is often forgotten. Webcomics have only recently been included in their native digital format within long-term preservation initiatives, such as those undertaken by the British Library (Aggleton 2019), the Library of Congress (Library of Congress 2014) and the Ivy Plus Libraries Confederation (Ivy Plus Libraries Confederation n.d.), but it is likely that the majority of webcomics are not yet covered by their remit.

When evaluated in its entirety, the webcomics communications circuit grants authors of self-published webcomics almost complete creative autonomy, the chance to establish direct contact with their audiences, freedom from the punishing deadlines of print comics, and an absence of gatekeepers that can bar entry into the field. The price to pay for such freedoms is, however, quite high. The absence of a publisher means no structure for regular remuneration, which can be offset only through a reliance on indirect and uncertain payments such as advertisements and crowdfunding. Additionally, self-hosted webcomics creators must undertake the potentially onerous activities of website maintenance and reader comment moderation, which have costs both in money and time. If they decide to print some of their creations, they must manage their printing and distribution workloads. Creators who rely on social media platforms for the hosting and distribution of their comics need to comply with their restrictions, which may constrain or ban certain types of content and reintroduce limits on their expression. The final and perhaps most significant challenge for independent webcomics creators is visibility, as authors cannot rely on established promotion mechanisms or on the prestige of specific publishers and have no clear avenues for emerging from within busy social media platforms.

1.5 Webtoons in Korea: Historical Context

The webtoon format of webcomics (see Section 1.2.3) originated in South Korea in the early 2000s as a result of a convergence of technological, social and economic factors. In the late twentieth century, the Korean comics market was dominated by natively produced *manhwa*, usually distributed to readers through *manhwabangs* stores specialising in lending rather than selling comics (Yecies and Shim 2021 p. 27). The existence of restrictions on *manhwa* content, such as the Juvenile Protection Act of 1997, and the elimination of import barriers in 1998 opened up the Korean market to the influx of Japanese manga, which proved extremely successful with readers (Kim 2022 p. 73). Coupled with the practice of *scanlation* (the illegal digitisation, online distribution and translation of manga), the South Korean comics industry suffered a series of severe blows. A number of technology start-ups in the 2000s began to develop systems and formats that would allow born-digital webcomics to be read and sold online. While the term 'webtoon' was coined by the search engine Chollian in 2000 (Yecies and Shim 2021 p. 5), it was the creation of the Daum Comics World platform in 2003 that marked 'a game changing moment' for the world of webtoons (Lee and In-Soo 2022), transforming it from amateur pastime into a commercially viable enterprise. The first longform webtoon, Kang Full's *Love Story*, was published on Daum to achieve over 60 million page views. A rival platform, Naver WEBTOON, was launched in 2005 by search engine Naver, quickly establishing itself as Daum's main competitor.

After initially viewing webtoons as loss leaders, Naver WEBTOON and Daum gradually 'aggregated audiences' to their webtoon portals (Kim and Yu 2019 p. 4). Monetisation strategies followed, with Daum introducing a 'pay-to-read' (Yecies and Shim 2021 p. 82) scheme for its most popular webtoons, including those created by Kang Full. Naver WEBTOON opted instead for a free-to-read approach funded through online advertisements, beginning in 2013 to share a percentage of advertisement revenue with webtoon creators (Kim and Yu 2019 p. 7).

The regulatory regime on comics was relaxed with the passing of the 2011 Promotion of Cartoons Act (Yecies and Shim 2021 p. 47), just as the advent of smartphones and their widespread diffusion, especially among teenagers and young adults, forced the reorientation of the Korean IT industry towards mobile services (Kim 2023 p. 422). Naver and Daum's webtoon portals too shifted towards mobile delivery. Daum's merger with mobile services company Kakao in 2014 allowed the newly formed

Daum/Kakao company to expand this strategy founded on *miribogi* micro-transactions (Cho 2021 p. 80) to include webnovels as well as webtoons. In parallel with these developments, the major webtoon portals all established their dedicated mobile apps as the main locus for the fruition and monetisation of their webtoon content in the early to mid 2010s. Daum/Kakao refined its monetisation strategy to a 'free-if-you-wait' approach, where older episodes of webtoons are released for free while newer ones can be unlocked through payment, while Naver WEBTOON introduced a similar 'Fast Pass' paid access for the most recent episodes of their comics, which then become free to read within 3–6 weeks of release.

The popularity of webtoons was also increased by several high-profile adaptations into K-drama television series and films on Korean channels such as tvN and JTBC and on streaming platforms such as Netflix for international audiences. Examples include Cho Gwang-jin's *Itaewon Class* (2016–18), serialised on Daum/Kakao, which was adapted into a critically acclaimed series distributed globally by Netflix, or *Yumi's Cells*, serialised by Lee Dong-gun on Naver WEBTOON in 2015–2020 and adapted by TVING in 2020. Other recent TV series adapted from WEBTOON and Daum/Kakao include horror titles such as *All of Us Are Dead*, *Sweet Home* and *Hellbound*, *Dr. Brain* for Apple TV+ and *True Beauty* for Rakuten Viki. The acquisition by WEBTOON of the online writing platform Wattpad in 2021 and by Daum/Kakao of the Tapas and Radish serialised content platforms has the explicit aim of creating content-production conglomerates that can facilitate this type of transmedia creative journey. A recent advertising campaign by WEBTOON (June 2022) focused explicitly on the multimedia nexus of webcomics, print and streaming, featuring slogans such as 'we're the story before it streams' (MacDonald 2022a). Adaptation of successful intellectual properties also flows in the opposite direction, with prominent webnovels such as *Solo Levelling*, released first on Daum/Kakao, being adapted into a webtoon series that has accrued over 14 billion page views and earned 'over £25 million in revenue' (Lee and In-Soo 2022), or the recently launched adaptation of TV series *Extraordinary Attorney Woo* into a webtoon hosted by WEBTOON (Yim 2022).

2 Diversity and Platformisation in Comics and Webcomics

The eyes of mainstream media are beginning to focus on the increased popularity of vertical-scrolling webtoons, as shown, for example, in global newspapers such as the *Financial Times* and the *New York Times* (Davies and Song 2022; Gustines and Stevens 2022). These news articles have identified the presence of a more diverse author base as one of the reasons for the international success of Korean webcomics such as those published by WEBTOON and Tapas. In order to assess the validity of these claims, this section first examines the profiles of US comics professionals and locates them within the landscape of English-language comics, including both US superhero comics and Japanese manga translations. As discussed in Section 1.3, the apparently monolithic communications circuit of US print comics is undergoing a series of transformations. It then examines the participation and role of female and nonbinary authors and readers in the communications circuits of comics and webcomics and delineates the impact of the 'platformisation' of cultural production into the latter (Cho 2021; Duffy et al. 2019; Kim and Yu 2019). Finally, this section asks whether the fluidity and openness of webcomics (Misemer 2021 pp. 218–9) are indeed enabling greater opportunities for readers and creators from certain marginalised communities (Hatfield 2015 p. 61; Misemer 2021 p. 220; Resha 2020 p. 70), discussing examples from US webcomics and comparing them to the operations of webtoon platforms.

2.1 Female Authors and Readers in US Comics and Manga

Comics are still perceived as associated with a 'predominantly heterosexual male authorship and readership' (Cocca 2016 p. 11). However, these views do not reflect in full either the history of English-language comics or its most recent developments. Work by comics scholars such as Trina Robbins and by projects such as 'She Changed Comics' by the Comic Book League Defense Fund have revealed the fundamental contributions of female comics creators across multiple periods and formats (Comic Book Legal Defense Fund 2015). These include female authors in genres that comprise action comics, such as Dale Messick and Tarpe Mills (Robbins 2013 pp. 63–4); romance comics, such as Ruth Atkinson and Lily Renée (Robbins 2013

p. 108); and superhero comics, including pioneers such as Marie Severin and Ramona Fradon (Robbins 2013 p. 120). Female creators have experimented with content and form outside mainstream comics publishing, for example, in feminist anthologies edited by Trina Robbins and Aline Kominsky amongst others; in influential independent comics, such as Wendy Pini's *Elfquest* (Robbins 2013 pp. 135–6); in expanding the genre of the graphic narrative autobiography, such as in works by Marjane Satrapi and Alison Bechdel (Chute 2010 p. 18); in gaining visibility and status within Japanese and global *manga*, for example, in the careers of Ryoko Ikeda, Moto Hagio and Rumiko Takahashi (Lunning 2015); and in employing webcomics to transform comics industries. Notable nonbinary and trans creators are also at the forefront of these movements, including authors such as Rachel Pollack, Jocelyn Samara (Hatfield 2015 p. 60), Maia Kobabe, Crystal Frasier and webcomic creators such as The Kao and Pseudonym Jones (Beat Staff 2022).

While it is difficult to quantify female and nonbinary authorship of webcomics, some attempts have been made for US print comics, which suggest that female and nonbinary participation in authorship is still far from equal. Published statistics for both authors and readers are even more difficult to find for traits that extend beyond gender identity, such as sexual orientation and ethnic background. This situation leads to an unfortunate flattening of diversity, with 'female' too often becoming synonymous with all non-male, non-white, non-cis and non-heterosexual workers in the comics industry. It is not the author's intention to elide these categories, which, moreover, are not mutually exclusive, but to acknowledge the limitations of existing scholarship and to define a field for the current study.

One report that does recognise LGBT+ creators is Benjamin Woo's survey of 570 comics professionals in the US, which he conducted in 2013–4. It reveals that at that point in the mid-2010s male creators still constituted 74.5 percent of the surveyed comics workforce. As well as being fewer in number (25.5 percent), female and nonbinary creators were more likely to be employed in more precarious, less remunerative roles. Woo also asked his respondents about their sexual orientation, revealing that 10 percent of male creators and 37.2 percent of female and nonbinary creators identified as homosexual, bisexual or other (Woo 2021 p. 13).

Besides this survey, quantifications of the gender composition of the comics workforce are limited at the moment to superhero publishers Marvel and DC. Tim Hanley's quarterly survey, the most recent of which is dated autumn 2020, evaluates that in October 2020, 35 percent of DC Comics (Hanley 2020a) and 30 percent of Marvel Comics (Hanley 2020b) published in those months included at least one female or nonbinary creator. To be noted, Hanley's definition of authorship is quite capacious and ranges to both writers and artists, including artists working on covers only, and to editors and assistant editors. In previous assessments, which employed a different methodology, Hanley measured that, on average, only 16.5 percent of DC and 16.3 percent of Marvel creators were female or nonbinary in the period January 2016 to March 2019. During this same period, these percentages never rose above 19.7 percent for DC and 18.8 percent for Marvel. Even if these far from equal distributions represent an improvement on the almost exclusively male (and white) comics world of the early 1990s (MacDonald 2020c), they nonetheless suggest that female and nonbinary creators are still a minority within the two largest US publishers of periodical comics.

This dispiriting picture must be balanced with evidence from comics publishers beyond DC and Marvel, who are making efforts to include a more diverse range of creators. For example, Image Comics from the 2010s have provided a platform for female creators working in genres beyond superheroes. Chief among them are creators such as artist Fiona Staples, the first woman to win the Eisner Award for Best Artist for *Saga* in 2015 and writer Marjorie Liu, the first woman to win the Eisner Award for Best Writer for *Monstress* in 2018. Image's creator-owned publication model, where authors retain the copyright of their comics, makes it more receptive to submissions from aspiring authors than its competitors, Marvel and DC. New publishers or publishing lines have also emerged that showcase female and nonbinary creators. Boom! Studios established its mark through comics aimed at an audience outside of the main male fan base, such as the Eisner-winning *Lumberjanes* (2014–20), the work of female, trans and nonbinary authors such as ND Stevenson, Grace Ellis, Shannon Watters and Kat Leyh. The Berger Books imprint of Dark Horse Comics, led by former DC editor Karen Berger, has published comics by established female creators coming from other comics publishers, such as G. Willow Wilson's *Invisible Kingdom*, Eisner Award winner for Best New Series in 2020, or from other media, such as Africanfuturism author Nnedi Okorafor's *LaGuardia*, winner of a Hugo Award and an Eisner Award in 2021. Other publishers such as IDW have also given prominence to female creators on their most prominent comics, such as the all-female teams led by Mairghread Scott on *Transformers* and Heather Nuhfer and Amy Mebberson on *My Little Pony* (2012–16). Even publishers specialising in superheroes such as DC and Marvel have begun to include more female creators, such as Gail Simone, Kelly Sue DeConnick, G. Willow Wilson, Kelly Thompson, Mariko Tamaki and Tini Howard. Editors such as Sana Amanat, co-creator with G. Willow Wilson of the Hugo Award-winning *Ms Marvel* and now Head of Content and Character Development at Marvel, are a further driver of change within superhero comics. Amanat and Marvel editors and authors, Ellie Pyle, Angélique Roché and Judy Stephens, for example, launched, in 2014, the *Women of Marvel* podcast series, which is also represented through well-attended panels at the most prominent comics conventions, including the San Diego and New York Comic Cons, and has a dedicated page on the official Marvel website (Marvel Comics n.d.).

It must be noted that despite these tentative signs of inclusion, female and nonbinary creators in superhero comics have contended with back-lashes from sections of the entrenched male fan base, who have protested vehemently against these perceived encroachments upon their territory and against the inclusion of more diverse characters in their favourite comics (Donnelly 2019). Certain male comics executives, such as Marvel's vice president of sales, David Gabriel, moreover, have in the past blamed declining sales numbers on publishers' attempts to increase the diversity of characters and readers (Cain 2017). The statistics mentioned above also obscure to an extent the vibrancy of comics created by nonbinary, gender-queer and trans creators, who are using comics and webcomics in particular to construct new spaces and communities (Galvan 2018 p. 433).

Looking beyond periodical comics, the advent in the English-speaking world of translations from Japanese manga comics also marked a decided shift in the number and visibility of more diverse creators. The US was a relative latecomer to the manga boom, which had already touched European comics markets such as Italy and France, as highlighted, for example, by Marco Pellitteri (2008 pp. 359–74). What differentiated English translations of manga quite markedly from superhero comics was their skipping of the periodical phase in the communications circuit to reach the public directly in graphic novel format. To be more precise, the periodical phase of manga comics takes place in the original Japanese context, where manga are serialised in short episodes through weekly or monthly periodicals. The most successful series are then collated into volumes known as *tankōbon* and go through a second circulation in book format. *Mangaka* authors generally work in small studios with teams of assistants, whom they pay through the fixed per-page remuneration received from manga periodicals during the serialisation of their titles. Such compensation is generally insufficient to cover all expenses, often exposing mangaka to serious financial strain (Sato 2013). Only if their comic is successful enough to warrant publication as a *tankōbon* do mangaka see their earnings increase, allowing them to secure a firmer financial status (Okeda 2019 p. 274). US manga publishers such as Tokyopop and Viz Media opted to translate *tankōbon* instead of periodicals and to distribute them through book trade channels rather than comics stores, especially 'bookstore chains' (Brienza 2016 pp. 52–8) such as Waldenbooks, Barnes and Nobles and Borders, the latter of which, until its demise in 2008, represented the main outlet for manga sales in the US market.

The very healthy comics sales of 2020 and 2021, especially in manga and graphic novels (Griepp 2022), suggest there is a public for comics written by more diverse creators, or that at least publishers are increasingly aware of the potential of what Henry Jenkins has labelled 'affective economics'. By providing products that 'commodify' the tastes of groups previously seen as marginal, cultural content industries can expand their market reach. In turn, the groups whose tastes are commodified, such a female comics readers, are exposed to a form of exploitation but also gain greater visibility within the industry (Jenkins 2006a pp. 61–2). For comics, publishers are attempting to respond to the expansion of a previously niche market by diversifying their offerings and addressing these new audiences (Resha 2020 p. 68). The diversification in terms of sales outlets is also benefiting female, nonbinary and marginalised readers, who are able to feel welcomed in comics communications circuits and to take active roles within them, especially in the case of webcomics (see below).

2.2 Female Readers and Authors in Webcomics

The audience of comics is, according to some studies, almost equally divided between male and female readers (Schenker 2021). However, female readers in mainstream US comics culture still report feeling 'stigmatised' (Orme 2016 p. 411) and excluded, or perceiving themselves as 'squatters' within the comics world (Cedeira Serantes 2019 p. 37). If the object of scrutiny shifts from liking comics to actually purchasing them, the percentage of female readers drops to 37 percent of the comics and graphic novels market (Alverson 2017). In some sections of the comics market, such as translated manga, female readers have, however, found content produced for an audience that is expected to be 'mostly female' or 'taking a female perspective', as testified by their composing 44 percent of manga buyers in 2017 (Alverson 2017). The perception of manga as valuing feminine perspectives is credited with positive psychological impacts (Erik-Soussi 2015 p. 25) on female participation in the whole US comics market. This involvement often begins within forums, social media and other locales for digital social reading (Pianzola 2021), which allow female and marginalised comics readers to configure themselves into a counterpublic that interrogates dominant discourses and media (Galvan and Misemer 2019 p. 2). Within webcomics, these counterpublics become part of 'correspondence zones' (Misemer 2019b p. 10) that involve readers in various roles in the communications circuit (see Section 1.4).

Because of the participatory circuits of webcomics (see Section1.2.2), a number of marginalised female and nonbinary readers are employing them to shift from consumer to producer, from 'object of looking' to 'creator of looking and sight' (Chute 2010 p. 2). The US and Japan differ in how this 'collective creativity' (Erik-Soussi 2015 p. 31) enters the communications circuit. In Japan, this happens primarily through *dōjinshi* fan comics, while in the US fanfiction, fan art and webcomics play a similar role. Self-published *dōjinshi* comics are a participatory medium that is particularly embraced by non-professional female creators, who can produce and distribute unconventional or innovative content outside the control of commercial publishers through specialised bookstores (Dahlan 2022 p. 7) and face-to-face conventions such as Komiket (Yasuda and Satomi 2019 pp. 268–71). Prominent female mangaka such as Rumiko Takahashi and the CLAMP collective launched thriving creative careers by debuting within *dōjinshi* that attracted mainstream publishers' attention, a route that enabled 'many female artists in the 1970s' to achieve publication (Orbaugh 2003 p. 116). *Dōjinshi* allow aspiring manga authors to inhabit a 'prosumer' space that is intermediate between amateurism and professionalism (Skains 2019 p. 5).

In the US, several noteworthy female and nonbinary creators have used webcomics as a pipeline for their emergence into the US comics publishing industries (Misemer 2021 p. 218) by demonstrating the existence of a public that did not fit with mainstream superhero publishing (Scott 2013 para. 2.4). The career of Faith Erin Hicks, for example, was significantly enhanced by her webcomic *Demonology 101* (Erik-Soussi 2015 p. 38). C. Spike Trotman was able to build upon her webcomic *Templar, Arizona*, to edit and crowdfund several comics anthologies, eventually establishing her own publishing company, Iron Circus Comics (Misemer 2021 p. 221). Webcomics have proved particularly empowering for marginalised creators, who have been able to use them to share content that addresses the concerns and reflects the perspectives of minoritized communities, such as members of the trans community (jackson and Stewart-Taylor 2020).

2.3 The Platformisation of the *WEBTOON* Communications Circuit

Such narratives of success must always be balanced by the uncertainties of webcomics communications circuits. The lack of gatekeepers does enable fluidity of content, styles and genres (Misemer 2021 p. 221), but the absence of a publishing infrastructure is reflected in the struggle of authors through multiple uncertain paths to financial sustainability (see Section 1.4). Korean webtoons have developed instead within a more structured trajectory from reader to amateur to professional creator through the expansion of webtoon platforms that exert control of every phase of the communications circuit.

Scholars indicate that 'platformisation' is the transformation of a limited number of content platforms 'from social network sites into social media platforms'. This process has caused social media to become 'the dominant infrastructural and economic model of the social web' (Helmond 2015 p. 1). Globally, the most influential content platforms are those owned by the so-called 'GAFAM' (Google, Apple, Facebook, Amazon and Microsoft) in the US and Europe, or by the 'three kingdoms' or 'BAT' (Baidu, Alibaba and Tencent) of the Chinese internet. Through their pervasiveness, these platforms shape content production into formats that are congenial to their drive for the collection and connection of web data, which has to be adapted for the platforms' format requirements in order to gain visibility and distribution through them (Helmond 2015). The cultural industries have also been affected by the same phenomena, as 'platform practices . . . shape cultural production' (Duffy et al. 2019 p. 2). Platforms such as YouTube, Twitch and TikTok are providing a stage for new and potentially more diverse creators and content to emerge, while at the same time monetising the free labour of the unpaid authors and viewers who upload, share and comment through the infrastructures they provide. As mentioned in Section 1.5, the most significant webtoon platforms in South Korea are Naver WEBTOON and Daum/Kakao. Together these portals and their monetisation, strategies have drastically changed how comics 'are perceived, consumed and understood' in South Korea (Cho 2021 p. 89). Parent companies Daum and Naver initially hosted webcomics as an addendum to their portals, which are part of their largely successful drive to achieve dominance in several market fields. Korean users of Daum and Naver, for example, can perform numerous daily tasks, such as web search, messaging, deliveries, as well as reading webtoons and web novels, through a single portal that offers multiple services. Most of them rely on insecurely employed gig workers (Kim 2023 p. 420) who receive limited remuneration while driving large profits for the parent companies.

This model has been extended to cultural fields such as webcomics production. The remarkable successes of webtoon platforms within the domestic Korean market have increased their visibility within public discourse. It has led to establishment of webcomics as 'one of the major cultural forms representing Korean youth culture' (Jin 2015). The recentring of the whole webtoon industry on a small number of platforms has enabled quasi-governmental institutions such as the Korea Creative Agency (KOCCA), the Korea Cartoonists Association and the Korean Manwha Contents Agency (KOMACON) (Cho 2021 pp. 85–7) to become actively involved in the shaping of webtoon production, for example, using them to channel funding provided through the 2012 Promotion of Cartoons Act (Yecies and Shim 2021 p. 72). The South Korean state has embraced webtoons as a valuable cultural output and as a fundamental component of the so-called '*hallyu*' or 'Korean Wave', which employs 'soft power' to promote Korean cultural and industrial outputs. At the time of writing, the Main Business section of KOCCA ranks comics third in its priority after Music and Games and ahead of Animation and Broadcasting (KOCCA Korea Creative Content Agency n.d.). Webtoons now form part of a multifaceted system with K-pop music, K-drama film and television, and a growing computer game and esports sector. It could be argued that webtoons have become, through platformisation, commodities that are appreciated by these Korean state agencies more for their economic than their cultural value (Cho 2021 p. 88).

Within this context, Naver WEBTOON decided to launch a US subsidiary, Line WEBTOON, in 2014. With the hope of increasing its reach in the American and European markets, Naver made the Los Angeles-based WEBTOON Entertainment 'the main unit for its webtoon business' (Park 2020), subordinating its flourishing Korean and Japanese subsidiaries to it in 2020. Now simply called WEBTOON, Naver's English-language arm has become one of the world's largest comics publishers (Stefanelli 2021). With these international subsidiaries for Naver WEBTOON and similarly for Daum/Kakao, webtoons ceased to be a primarily Korean phenomenon and began to acquire visibility in United States and European news outlets (Davies and Song 2022; Gustines and Stevens 2022). Both companies have invested heavily in English-language webtoons, both translated from Korean and original, and have established an English-language webtoon communications circuit that is located in its entirety within the platform, like its Korean antecedents. WEBTOON's strategy comprises all the key elements that the webcomics communications circuit shares with the fields of self-publishing and fanfiction (Ramdarshan Bold 2018; Skains 2019), such as micropayments, participatory audience engagement mechanisms and the opportunity for readers to become creators, but deploys them within a platformisation model (Kim and Yu 2019).

As currently configured (2022), the English-language WEBTOON platform comprises two sections: a hosting platform named WEBTOON Canvas and a selection of curated comics, known as WEBTOON Originals, that are produced by creators who are in receipt of regular payments from WEBTOON. The subsections below will analyse in greater depth the operations of WEBTOON Canvas and WEBTOON Originals.

2.3.1 WEBTOON Canvas

In the self-publishing WEBTOON Canvas section, authors retain all rights to their creations and can host them for free, with the right to also publish them simultaneously in other venues, such as the rival Tapas portal, owned by Daum/Kakao. Comics are uploaded in episodes comprising a variable number of panels and experienced by readers through a web browser or through the dedicated WEBTOON mobile app. These portals allow users to read WEBTOON Canvas comics without payment, as detailed in Section 1.4.2. A small, relatively unobtrusive ad is placed at the bottom of each issue, generating revenue that is shared with creators through WEBTOON's Ad Revenue Sharing programmes (see below). Past issues of each series remain available on WEBTOON Canvas for perusal while the comic is being actively serialised on the platform.

Through platforms such as WEBTOON Canvas and Tapas Community, aspiring creators can showcase their visions to a potentially global audience and develop their skills, building a community of readers and supporters (see Section 1.4). While WEBTOON Canvas can be seen as an example of the digital evolution of participatory cultures, where 'every reader [is] understood to be a potential writer' (Jenkins 2006b p. 144), the platform both enables and exploits their desire to share their content and to grow a career out of their creativity. By WEBTOON's own evaluation, '75% of readers are Gen Z and younger Millennials; around 60% of users are female' (WEBTOON 2023a). This predominantly young and female audience form a pool of non-professional creators that the platform develops through an 'artist incubating system' (Cho 2021 p. 83). The most successful of the amateur webcomics they upload, as evaluated through a combination of reader engagement metrics and editorial judgement, are promoted by the platform through a two-tier structure. This fundamental step within the WEBTOON circuit is achieved through the built-in reader feedback mechanisms, such as likes, ratings and comments. The platform does not need to search through other social media to gauge the popularity of a webtoon; its readers provide it for free with metrics and feedback. These data are used by WEBTOON to measure the success of each title and to position Canvas creators into different 'tiers' with incremental remuneration from advertisements (Lamerichs 2020 p. 223). At the most basic level, WEBTOON measures weekly page views. Further up in the engagement scale is the reader's ability to 'like' an episode, followed by the ability to 'subscribe' to a title, receiving an alert whenever a new episode is published, and to rate a series from 1 to 10 stars (see Section 3.4, where these measures are discussed in more detail). Finally, readers can comment on each episode and either 'upvote' or 'downvote' other readers' comments or reply to them. The three most upvoted comments appear at the top of the comments roll with the label 'Top comment', which is prized by dedicated readers. Issues can have a variable number of comments, ranging from a handful to tens of thousands. Authors can reply to comments but have only recently acquired the ability to moderate them (WEBTOON 2021). WEBTOON itself exercises no moderation on comments except for prohibiting 'abusive or hateful' content and comments in its Community Policy (WEBTOON 2022a). It leaves authors to address the burden of policing their own community, which is a source of complaints and tensions, especially when hateful comments are addressed to authors from marginalised backgrounds. Such a situation is not uncommon on other platforms that capitalise on reader feedback such as Goodreads (McCluskey 2021). Additionally, the algorithmic basis of the calculations WEBTOON uses to assess popularity is not transparent but more akin to a black box, leaving question marks over its exact functioning and, potentially, its fairness (Murray 2021 p. 976).

It can be assessed that WEBTOON Canvas delivers the most significant functions of a comics platform (hosting, reader engagement, archiving), relieving its creators of the burden of technical maintenance. Moreover, it provides authors with regular updates on the reach of their comics through the same metrics described above that are used to gauge the commercial viability of a series. Canvas creators who achieve 1,000 subscribers and 40,000 global monthly page views can apply to join the platform's Ad Revenue Sharing Program (www.webtoons.com/en/creators101/make-money), which provides creators with 50 percent of net ad revenue. In addition, Canvas comics that achieve 200,000 global monthly page views can apply for the Reward Ads programme, whereby readers who want preview access to the latest episode of a series can do so by watching a short 30-second video ad. This additional revenue is welcomed by authors such as Cecilia, author of *Lemon Soda and Coffee* on WEBTOON Canvas, as explained in an interview for the *Pixels and Panels* podcast (n.d.). A further programme, the 2022 Canvas Creator Rewards, grants further monthly payments from $100 to $1,000, though its sliding scale of global monthly page views requirements, ranging from 40,000 to 1,500,000, limits the number of series that can benefit from the highest reward tiers. A new system based on tipping is slated to be implemented in 2023 to replace the Creator Rewards programme (www.webtoons.com/en/notice/detail?noticeNo=2390).

At first sight, publishing on Canvas may appear quite advantageous to creators, but there are trade-offs in exchange for access to the platform. By devolving publishing functions to WEBTOON, creators limit certain of the benefits of the webcomics communications circuit, such as absolute freedom of content and direct collaboration with their audience. Both trade-offs can potentially hamper novice authors, especially if they are female, nonbinary or LGBT+. Firstly, Canvas creators must comply with WEBTOON's Community Policy, which, for example, forbids content that has sexual gratification as its sole objective and content that incites hatred (WEBTOON 2022a). Secondly, authors must provide two genre labels for their comics, fitting it within the limited range of a predefined taxonomy (WEBTOON n.d.-b). Thirdly, ad revenue alone is usually insufficient to support a creator as a sole source of income, even for those Canvas creators that are accepted into the additional revenue programmes. Most Canvas authors therefore resort to crowdfunding platforms such as Patreon in order to integrate their income. Apart from free hosting and the potential ad revenue, Canvas creators receive no other direct support from WEBTOON, a situation that can disadvantage novice and diverse authors.

However, the biggest drawback to WEBTOON Canvas is, paradoxically, its own success. Such are the visibility and appeal of the platform that it now contains, by the account of its North America CEO Ken Kim, '130 K CANVAS stories' (Salkowitz 2021). While the popularity of the WEBTOON platform brings millions of potential readers to it, it can be difficult for individual comics to emerge. The searchability of Canvas is also limited, with no possibility to filter results through, for example, a combination of multiple genre tags. Diverse comics, such as those with an LGBT+ focus like 'Boys' Love' (BL) or 'Girls' Love' (GL) webcomics, cannot even be tagged as such, languishing instead in crowded genres such as 'Romance' or 'Fantasy' (see Section 3.5 for a discussion of genres in WEBTOON). This is not the case for popular manga publishers such as Kodansha (https://kodansha.us/), which includes genre labels like 'LGBT', 'Yaoi/BL' and 'Yuri/GL'. WEBTOON's most direct competitor, Tapas, also allows comics to be filtered by 'BL', 'GL' and 'LGBTQ+' tags. WEBTOON Canvas employs instead more algorithmic and hence somewhat more opaque search mechanisms that suggest new series based on readers' previous content choices and other unspecified criteria. Lists of 'Popular by Genre' comics are available, but they tend to privilege established series, with higher numbers of readers and subscribers, hence relegating new Canvas series to a position of limited visibility. Canvas creators attempt to remedy these shortcomings of the platform by recommending each other's series, either at the end of weekly instalments or through social media. In such a busy space, new Canvas authors who arrive onto the platform without a pre-existing community of readers often struggle to be noticed. Furthermore, the inability of creators and readers to tag and search for LGBT+ webtoons obscures, to an extent, their presence within WEBTOON.

One escape route from this limited visibility is through the platforms' use of 'competition crowdsourcing' (Kim and Yu 2019 p. 7), where the amateur creators on Canvas vie with one another for the chance to become webtoon professionals by publication on WEBTOON Originals.

WEBTOON staff monitor the Canvas content pool in search of promising authors, basing their evaluation on a combination of 'technical analysis . . . number of users . . . [and] insight of producer and editors' (Salkowitz 2021). These Canvas creators are recruited either through a direct call from the WEBTOON Originals editors or through periodical competitions focused on eliciting contributions in specific genres, such as the recent 'Call to Action' competition (WEBTOON 2022b). Such competitions usually offer a cash prize and a publishing deal in the WEBTOON Originals section to the selected winners. The WEBTOON Canvas structure presents opportunities for the authors and platforms, who can both benefit from investment in comics series capable of achieving a high level of audience engagement. Arguably though, the system primarily favours the platform, which benefits from the traffic generated by the large amounts of webtoons produced at no cost by amateur creators. Overall, little or no remuneration goes to the majority of these amateur authors on Canvas, who thus provide their creative labour for free through a form of 'work volunteerism' (Kim and Yu 2019 p. 6) that potentially devalues their contribution. This view is confirmed to an extent by a recent ad campaign by WEBTOON, which labelled comics as 'literature's fun side-hustle' (MacDonald 2022a), seemingly belittling both webtoons and creators. Given the audience breakdown mentioned above, it is likely that most of the Canvas creators struggling to break into Originals are young and female.

2.3.2 WEBTOON Originals

The WEBTOON Originals section of WEBTOON differs from Canvas in containing elements that bring it closer to the operations of a publisher, albeit an entirely digital one. In exchange for granting WEBTOON exclusive rights to publish their content for a number of years, authors on WEBTOON Originals receive regular monthly compensation, free hosting for their series, the support of an editor, and marketing promotion through the WEBTOON social media presence. Similarly to Canvas creators, WEBTOON Originals authors can also receive a share of advertisement revenue and are able to maintain additional income streams such as Patreon accounts and online shops. WEBTOON Originals comics are free to read for the final user, either on the web or through the dedicated WEBTOON mobile app. In an extension of the 'free-if-you-wait' approach pioneered on their Korean platform (see Section 1.5), a variable number of episodes, usually 3–6, are available for advance viewing or 'Fast Pass' (FP) in exchange for a fee in the form of an in-app currency called 'coins'. The current price of 'coins' at the time of writing is 10 coins for $0.99, with new episodes of the most popular series having recently increased to 7 coins per episode from the earlier 5, amidst reader complaints of inflation. As well as discovering plot developments in advance, readers who purchase Fast Passes usually monopolise the 'Top comments' section, which amounts, according to Lamerichs, to the concentration of 'a form of status' in the hands of readers with greater financial means (2020 p. 223). A form of self-censorship is expected of Fast Pass readers, who are asked not to reveal the storyline developments they are privy to in the comments, which are open to all readers. Fast Pass revenue is shared with authors once a minimum threshold of purchases has been reached, though this revenue-generating process and the transparency of its accounting have been the subject of recent controversy (see Section 4 later in this section). Within the WEBTOON app but not the web interface, WEBTOON Originals readers may download several issues to their device for offline reading, subject to a maximum retention period of 30 days. They are not allowed to redistribute the downloaded comics outside of the platform.

With WEBTOON Originals, authors are bound to upload a minimum number of panels, which varies according to individual contracts, as explained by Leanne Krecic. The creator of *Let's Play* reports that there are 'some creators [who] have 30 panels a week and others whose count goes up to 100' (2022). Most authors publish at regular weekly or even bi-weekly intervals, with the latter frequency often employed by authors who work in the Comedy or Slice of Life genres, while those active within Romance, Fantasy or Drama comics usually opt for longer weekly instalments (see Section 3.5 for a discussion of genres in WEBTOON). Such a publishing schedule is regarded by authors as quite onerous, especially given that WEBTOON creators are likely to be working alone, instead of being surrounded by a team of co-authors, as in US comics, or assistants, as in manga. The majority of webtoon authors in Korea have little or no prior expertise in publication, unlike in the traditional *manhwa* industry, where junior artists usually begin as apprentices and are expected to practice 'self-study' in order to improve (Kim and Yu 2019 p. 3). The significance of the expected time commitments for WEBTOON Originals authors has been described as 'one of the most startling factors' for creators used to the production schedules of US comics (Krecic (Mongie) 2022). Only the most successful ones are able to employ assistants, who are usually credited at the end of each weekly episode but only more rarely billed as co-authors. Authors are allowed to take a break from the publishing schedule of their comic but forego remuneration during the hiatus period. In addition, authors fear losing audience during a hiatus, as comics that are not currently published are ranked lower in the WEBTOON charts and risk losing to new series all but the most dedicated readers and subscribers.

As well as comics created specifically for the US WEBTOON platform, the curated content in WEBTOON Originals also includes several translations from the most prominent Korean WEBTOON titles, such as *Tower of God*, *True Beauty* and *The God of High School*. In total, Korean translations comprise 424 out of 825 WEBTOON Originals present on the platform when this study was conducted, or 51 percent. These titles and their translations can be seen as attempts to monetise abroad content that has proven very lucrative domestically, as is the case with titles such as *True Beauty* and *The God of High School*. At the same time, the English-language WEBTOON Originals also include numerous comics that have never been published before in any language. When entering this arena, WEBTOON under Head of Content Tom Akel initially featured 'a mix of US comics stars' with an established profile in US print comics (MacDonald 2018), such as Warren Ellis, Dean Haspiel, Fabian Nicieza and Marvel founder Stan Lee. Some of the resulting series achieved critical distinction, such as Dan Schkade's *Lavender Jack* (2017–2023), which was nominated for an Eisner Award in 2019. During 2018, however, Akel was removed from his position as WEBTOON opted for a different model, which relied on translations and on developing user-generated series that emerged from competition crowdsourcing on Canvas.

At the time of writing, WEBTOON Originals publishes comics by 694 first-named authors, plus 306 second- and third-named authors. Of these, currently ongoing series account for 443 first authors and 213 secondary or

tertiary ones. In an interview published in 2015, when the English-language
WEBTOON platform was only one year old, WEBTOON founder Jun-
Koo Kim stated that WEBTOON could offer monthly payments 'starting
at \$2,000 a month', while adding that certain Korean creators were able to
achieve 'upwards of \$80,000 a month' through advertising revenue (Cabeal
2015). The shift in the publication venue of such interviews, from niche
comics blogs in 2015 to the *New York Times* in 2022 is a mark of the
increased visibility of WEBTOON among English-language media.

Even if Kim's words had the objective of presenting the new platform in
the best possible light, the opportunities for the highest-earning creators
seem to have been confirmed in more recent surveys. The most successful
Korean webcomic creators are reported to be earning revenues ranging
from hundreds of thousands to even millions of dollars. According to
WEBTOON, their (unnamed) top-earning Korean creator achieved an
income of '12.4 billion won in 2021', equivalent to a staggering
\$9.5 million dollars (Yoon 2022a). The company put the average annual
income of a Korean WEBTOON creator at 280 million won (\$212,000),
with even new authors achieving 150 million won (\$114,000) in their
first year. These salaries are even more remarkable when considering the
young age of Korean webtoon creators, with 'a combined 83.9 percent'
being in their 20s and 30s (Korea Times 2021).

These significant incomes for authors are made possible by the increasing global revenues of the WEBTOON platform, which surpassed 1 trillion
won in 2020, achieving the equivalent of \$843 million in 2020 and
\$900 million in 2021 sales. Both are substantial amounts when considering
that the aggregate income of the entire US comics industry was \$1.4 billion
in 2020 and \$2.075 billion in 2021, the best ever year for comics sales, as
shown in Section 1.1. Yet according to recent estimates, only a fraction of
this amount reaches creators, leaving many to struggle with uncertain
wages and 'disadvantageous contract issues' (Kim and Lee 2022). The
situation is even more complex for non-Korean creators. Over the period
2020–2021, WEBTOON US paid its English-language creators \$27 million,
an increase of 75 percent compared to 2019 figures. These apparently
generous amounts need to be compared to the much higher earnings for
Korean creators mentioned above. If the figure of \$212,000 is accepted as the

average remuneration of a Korean WEBTOON creator, the company would appear to be paying its 700 signed Korean creators a higher proportion of its annual gross take than its US branch. Creators that sign contracts with WEBTOON subsidiaries in Latin America are allegedly paid even lower rates (see Section 4). The most substantial beneficiary in this communications circuit, at least in monetary terms, remains the platform, which is able to transform the free labour of amateur creators and the clicks and attention of readers into profit.

2.4 Evaluation

Webcomics have served as a springboard for the professional careers of numerous female, nonbinary and LGBT+ creators, thanks to the counterpublics and correspondence zones that are enabled by the expressive freedoms of the medium. WEBTOON authors, especially beginners, inhabit a space that is suspended between amateurism and professionalism. They are likely to have emerged from the ranks of an increasingly diverse comics-reading public and have taken their first steps to authorship through webcomics and free hosting platforms such as WEBTOON Canvas. They have sacrificed some of the affordances of a fully independent webcomics circuit, such as complete expressive freedom and a direct relationship with their public. In exchange, they may have obtained a more regular remuneration and the potential to be seen by an audience that numbers in the millions and extends to the whole globe. Can this relentless process of platformisation help more diverse creators and comics to emerge?

Section 3 identifies the most successful comics on WEBTOON Originals and examines their genre, comparing them to US print comics. It discusses and quantifies the gender breakdown of the most popular WEBTOON Originals authors and asks whether the WEBTOON platform, despite its control on the webtoon communications circuit, still promotes creativity and offers opportunities for more diverse creators. Do webtoons still open up 'new spaces for expressions' (Duffy et al. 2019 p. 3), even when the fluidity and openness of webcomics is channelled through a corporate platform?

3 Female and Nonbinary Authors in WEBTOON Originals

Scholars are currently debating whether platformisation actually 'enables more diversity in cultural producers in terms of gender, sexual identity, race, ethnicity, age, and social class' (Cunningham & Craig 2019 pp. 184–187; Duffy et al. 2019 p. 4). A full exploration of these questions is not possible within the limits of this study, but the metrics that WEBTOON employs to assess the popularity of webtoons are published on their website. When analysed and interpreted, they can indicate which webtoon genres attract the highest number of readers and help identify the most read authors. In turn, their gender identities can be counted and assessed in comparison with other segments of the comics industry.

3.1 Introduction: The WEBTOON Disruption

This study argues that one of the most significant innovations brought by webtoon publishers, such as WEBTOON and Tapas/Kakao, lies in their enabling a select number of female and nonbinary creators to achieve commercial success, or at least in providing a potential path to do so. While platforms such as WEBTOON and Tapas/Kakao do impose certain of the controls that are typical of publishers, such as content restrictions in the comics they publish, their heuristics are not identical to those of US superhero comics. There are no established celebrity authors (yet) in webtoons, no characters or titles that are guaranteed to attract millions of readers. Decisions on whether to contract or promote a title depend, ostensibly, on an author's success in engaging an audience, as measured through a combination of audience metrics (see Section 2.3.1). In order to understand the 'author incubation' system that is integral to platformisation, a range of these measurements, such as page views, likes, subscriptions and ratings, will be used by this study to attempt a quantification of diversity of gender and genre in WEBTOON Originals.

This section focuses on WEBTOON in its position as the largest English-language platform for webtoons. The digital availability of webtoons allows the use of a combination of qualitative methods based on close reading and quantitative ones based on larger-scale data collection to address certain research questions. Data on readership and engagement is shared publicly by WEBTOON on its own platform, providing apparently greater immediacy than the sales figures released for print comics, which are filtered through intermediaries such as Diamond Comic Distributors or Circana Bookscan (formerly Nielsen Bookscan). A recent change in Terms and Conditions for WEBTOON (WEBTOON 2023b), however, prohibits data acquisition from their site through automated means such as webscraping, which casts a question mark over future availability of this type of data for research (see Section 3.2.1 and Section 4 for further discussion).

Section 3 analyses and interprets the data gathered from WEBTOON Originals on over 800 comics. It adopts this 'meso' scale (Murray 2022) as arguably the most appropriate lens for balancing concerns of representativeness and reproducibility with a Humanities and Book History focus on in-depth studies. It does so by discussing the entire research process, from research modelling to data collection, data cleaning, structuring and analysis to interpretation and evaluation.

The figures reported in market analyses of US print comics such as *Batman* or *Spider-Man*, which reach monthly sales in the hundreds of thousands, are for individual instalments of ongoing comics. Multiplying monthly figures by 12 months suggests that the most successful superhero comics achieve yearly 'page views' of over one billion. Mid-range comics such as Marvel's *Spider-Gwen: Gwenverse* (2022), with estimated monthly sales of around 48,000 in April 2022 (Comichron 2022), still accrue yearly sales of millions of copies. The equivalent page views achieved by 825 WEBTOON Originals comics are cumulative over the 8 years the platform has been in operation. Their total numbers, as will be shown below, must be examined within this context. When it is remembered that the majority of the WEBTOON titles are by newcomers to the English-language market, the noteworthiness of their achievement is, however, increased. It is extremely unlikely, for example, that new and untested creators, especially if female or nonbinary, would be entrusted with authoring the most popular superhero comics such as *Batman* or *Spider-Man*. It is more probable that they would begin with titles from a smaller publisher that is open to diverse authors, such as Boom! Studios or IDW. These would have lower monthly sales, and therefore monthly page views in the low tens of thousands or low hundreds of thousands on a yearly basis. Such series would operate in a somewhat more precarious space, with lower remuneration and a more uncertain future.

The WEBTOON Originals homepage (https://www.webtoons.com/en/dailySchedule) lists all the comics that WEBTOON has published under this imprint. They are divided between 'Ongoing' and 'Completed' Series. Ongoing Series are presented in further subdivisions by day of weekly publication. At the date of scraping in the third quarter of 2022, WEBTOON Originals was hosting a total of 825 series, of which 360 were 'Completed' and the remaining 465 were ongoing. The extremely rapid addition of new series makes the task of monitoring and quantifying WEBTOON and its practices quite complex, potentially requiring frequent resampling. For example, in a previous sampling conducted in 2021, WEBTOON Originals was hosting a total of 598 series, with therefore a year-on-year increase of over 200 series. The totals used in this Element are based on a survey conducted in autumn 2022, subject to the Disclaimer at the start of this Element.

The focus on quantitative metrics provides for only indirect analyses of readers' experiences. Within Darnton's theorisation of the print communications circuit, readers were identified as the most 'mysterious' agent to assess (Darnton 1982 p. 80). The same digitisation and platformisation processes that centralise the webtoon communications circuit now make it increasingly possible to capture readers' experiences and voices. Comments within WEBTOON and in forums or social media could provide rich sources of evidence to be analysed with digital humanities methodologies (Rebora and Pianzola 2018; Pianzola et al. 2020) within the framework of a theorisation of the comments section of webtoons (Misemer 2021 p. 220). However, in addition to the restrictions imposed by the WEBTOON Terms of Use (see Section 3.2.1), ethical issues must be addressed when capturing comments through bulk methods such as webscraping. The collection of comments could accidentally expose personal and sensitive data, as defined by the legislation such as the General Data Protection Regulations (European Parliament 2016), which include characteristics such as the religious beliefs, sexual orientation and location of the commenter. Moreover, it is not possible to judge prior to data collection whether any comment has been posted by users falling into protected categories, such as minors or readers with disabilities. Comments on WEBTOON, as on many online platforms, are pseudonymous, but it is arguable that, with concerted efforts, users could be de-anonymised from the content and timing of their comments. One way to avoid these issues would be to hand-pick comments that refer to the reading experience, but to do so would inevitably introduce issues of sample bias. Bulk webscraping queries would need to be carefully constructed and filtered for personal information before analysing the obtained data. Additionally, while quantitative methods such as sentiment analysis could bring rich fruit, qualitative approaches are also needed, such as interviews and focus groups (Cedeira Serantes 2019 p. 23), especially when examining the significance of webtoons for LGBT+ readers. This approach requires more time for design, execution and evaluation than is available for the present study. Such research on the readers of webtoons constitutes an ideal follow-up to this study and can address in greater depth the complex issues of gender and identity that the present digitally focused methods cannot do full justice to.

3.2 Research Design

The first step in every research process is always to clearly define its scope. As mentioned in Section 1, WEBTOON is divided into two sections, Originals and Canvas. The latter is even more volatile than the former. The self-published series it hosts show extreme variance in length, frequency of publication and readership, ranging from worldwide successes such as Alice Oseman's *Heartstopper*, with a readership in the millions, to more niche series with a few thousand or even a few hundred readers. The Originals section was therefore preferred as both more stable and more representative of WEBTOON's practices as a cultural content platform. Originals further offer the advantage of a single index page (www.webtoons.com/en/dailySchedule) where all series are presented simultaneously, making the task of acquiring data more streamlined.

3.2.1 WEBTOON Terms of Use

Before any data was collected, it was deemed necessary to undertake a Research Ethics assessment with the author's research ethics office, which was carried out and approved during 2022 (project reference

HREC/4496/Benatti). The review by The Open University's Human Research Ethics Committee (HREC) stipulated that, while the data that was going to be collected presented no ethical implications, permission must be obtained from WEBTOON before proceeding. As suggested by HREC, the author attempted to contact the WEBTOON Intellectual Property and Press email addresses three times over a period of one month but received no reply. A good faith effort was deemed to have been conducted, and the research was allowed to proceed by The Open University's HREC.

In June 2023, just as this study was undergoing peer review, WEBTOON updated its Terms of Use to explicitly prohibit the 'unauthorized "crawling," "scraping," or harvesting of content or personal information, or use any other unauthorized automated means to compile information available through the Services' (WEBTOON 2023b). All data collection was conducted prior to the new Terms of Use, but nonetheless the author contacted WEBTOON to inform them of this upcoming publication. The WEBTOON Intellectual Property office, while interested in this study, did not initially concede their approval for the use of these webscraped data. After extended negotiations involving The Open University's IP office, WEBTOON eventually allowed this study to proceed, on the basis of the data collected in 2022 before the Terms update and subject to the Disclaimer included at the beginning of this Element. The data that is analysed here must be assessed as solely reflective of the WEBTOON US platform and as a snapshot of a particular moment in time.

The research process described below is included for transparency, but it should not be followed by other researchers without prior engagement with WEBTOON and with their institution's ethical and legal team.

3.2.2 Webscraping

Data was captured using the Webscraper.io tool (https://webscraper.io/). While programming languages such as Python including packages for webscraping, Webscraper.io proved sufficient for the task at hand. Scraped data for each WEBTOON Originals series included both bibliographical-style metadata and markers of reader engagement.

The metadata markers included:

- Title
- Author(s)
- Genre
- URL

The reader engagement markers comprised:

- Number of page views
- Number of 'Likes'
- Number of subscriptions
- Average reader rating (on a scale from 1 to 10)

A further possible measure, the number of published episodes for each series, could also be considered as a proxy of popularity with readers, as titles that are less successful tend to be terminated, whether at the creator's or the publisher's instigation. However, a straightforward appraisal of the number of episodes per series was discarded due to the difficulty of quantifying the length of the Completed series. This apparent contradiction is due to WEBTOON's 'Day Pass' practice, whereby selected Completed series are re-released one episode per day, with no more than 14 episodes being available at any given time, unless readers purchase permanent access. The approach results in a further source of income for authors, but also in certain Completed series displaying an artificially reduced number of episodes, which renders this measure difficult to gauge. Even if a series is selected for Day Pass, previously accrued page views, likes and subscribers are not erased, making these measures more stable and reliable.

3.2.3 Data Cleaning

The second phase of the research was data cleaning. Webscraper.io provided consistent data, but the steps involved in the webscraping resulted in the collection of duplicate data, such as the comics' URL, as well as the combination of several pieces of data (Genre, Title, Author, and Likes) in a single field. Acquired data was therefore exported in .csv format and imported into OpenRefine, a free tool originally developed by Google for working with untidy data (https://openrefine.org/). The cleaning phase involved splitting some of the scraped data into separate columns for easier quantification in later stages of the study. No data was added in OpenRefine apart from labelling the columns created when splitting fields. The cleaned data was then exported in .csv format and ingested into Microsoft Excel, where it was saved in .xlsx format.

De-duplication of results was carried out within Microsoft Excel. While the vast majority of Originals series are published only once a week, a few, especially in the Comedy and Slice of Life genres, are published more frequently, either twice or three times per week. For the purposes of this study, all duplicate occurrences of the same series were identified and removed, leaving only one instance for each individual series. A total of 29 duplicate entries were therefore removed from the 854 recorded with Webscraper.io, leaving 825 distinct series between Ongoing and Completed comics. Further data cleaning steps involved transforming WEBTOON's shorthand notation, which uses 'M' for 'million' and 'B' for 'billion' into a numerical format that could be analysed using Excel's built-in Pivot Tables.

The data about the WEBTOON Originals series can be ranked and analysed through several approaches. For example, WEBTOON classifies the 'popularity' of its comics through a combination of measures, as explained in the rules for the recent 'Call to Action' contest, which mentions evaluating entries through a combination of number of 'views, likes, and comments' (https://www.webtoons.com/en/notice/detail?noticeNo=2572). The evaluation of the content of comments would appear at first sight to yield potential results for studying reader engagement, but these must be weighed against the restrictions mentioned above (see Section 3.1). This study is therefore based on fully anonymous metrics such as Page views, Likes and Subscriptions, where it is not possible to connect an action to a specific user without being granted access to WEBTOON's own logs and records, which this researcher is not privy to.

3.2.4 Korean Translations in WEBTOON Originals

The data selection for WEBTOON Originals is further complicated by the publisher's reliance, at the present moment, on translations from Korean of series that have proven successful on its parent platform, Naver WEBTOON. As discussed previously (see Section 1.5), these translated series originate from a webcomics ecosystem that does not directly compete with the English-language milieu inhabited by DC and Marvel comics and is better compared instead with other comics in translation, such as manga. The inclusion of translations of previously published content represents indeed one further commonality between WEBTOON Originals and manga. One difference to be noted is that, in the case of manga publishers, translations tend to comprise the majority of their offerings, though original English language or global manga is rapidly expanding (Brienza 2016 pp. 67–8). The WEBTOON Originals platform too encompasses an inter-mixture or both translations and content directly published in English. Translated webtoons include some of the most liked series, such as *Tower of God*, *True Beauty* and *Lookism*, with audiences in the hundreds of millions. However, what this study wants to assess primarily is whether the arrival of WEBTOON into the English-language comics market is providing content of more varied genres to an English-language readership and creating opportunities for female and nonbinary creators. Titles translated from Korean are useful to address the first part of the question, since readers can approach them in the same way as content written originally in English. But for the second part of the question, only titles that are not translated from Korean were considered. The most successful translated comics can reach a wider public in an English-language context, but only after they have undergone a further step in editorial assessment and a further transformation through translation in another language. An in-depth focus on comics primarily written in English for an English-language audience was therefore chosen.

Therefore, a derived dataset of the 80 'most popular' comics were created with the aim of researching the gender of the authors of this subset. Hence, it was necessary to establish measures that could represent reader numbers and engagement. The sections below discuss the four measures of engagement (views, likes, subscriptions and ratings) and their roles in the further steps of the analysis. The WEBTOON Originals series were then ranked by number of page views, likes and subscriptions received. The full dataset is available in .csv and Excel formats in the Supplementary Material and from the author upon request. The main figures for the whole dataset are summarised in Table 1.

Table 1. Summary measures for the WEBTOON Originals dataset.

Total WEBTOON Originals comics	825
Total Page Views	33,107,087,944
Total Likes	2,536,089,996
Total Subscribers	373,463,908

3.3 Genre Classification

The first area where WEBTOON Originals, in its role as a publisher, ushers in new possibilities for authors is in the embracing of a wider range of genres compared to mainstream US print comics such as those published by DC and Marvel. Within WEBTOON Originals, series are labelled with a single Genre chosen from a controlled vocabulary that includes sixteen options. By contrast, Canvas authors can choose two Genre descriptors. It is not specified whether for Originals this choice is imposed by WEBTOON or whether authors have an input or can request changes. The sixteen Originals genres are represented in Table 2, which includes the number of series that are thus classified. Genres are used on WEBTOON Originals to help readers navigate through the site. A 'Genres' tab is present in the main page navigation menu, grouping series that share a common classification. Certain genres (Mystery, Sports, Historical, Heartwarming, Horror and Informative) are hidden behind a further 'Others' tab, thus becoming less visible to readers.

Unlike US periodical print comics, where 'Superhero' is predominant, among WEBTOON Originals 'Fantasy' and 'Romance' are the leading genres. They are followed by 'Drama' and 'Action', and subsequently by more comedy-oriented genres such as 'Comedy' and 'Slice of Life'. 'Superhero' comics comprise only 30 titles or 3.7 percent of the total 825 series. This contrasts sharply with the continued ascendancy of the genre in the main US publishers such as DC and Marvel. To find other genres in US print comics, such as Sci-fi, Fantasy or Slice of Life, readers must explore the catalogues of smaller publishers, such as Image, Dark Horse and Boom!

Table 2. WEBTOON Originals comics divided by Genre.

Genre	WEBTOON Originals by Genre
Fantasy	151
Romance	139
Drama	94
Action	93
Comedy	64
Slice of Life	56
Thriller	49
Supernatural	43
Sci-fi	40
Superhero	30
Horror	25
Mystery	14
Sports	13
Informative	7
Historical	5
Heartwarming	2

Studios, or choose among the range of manga genres that WEBTOON Originals most closely resembles. It must be remarked that, while a range of series are available in the offerings of the abovementioned US publishers, from within their websites comics are not searchable by genre, but only by author or title, in sharp contrast with manga publishers such as Viz or Kodansha (see Section 4 for evaluation). Webcomics from the Korean platform are also distinctive when compared to the early webcomics described in Section 1.3, which tended to feature short, humorous episodes. WEBTOON Originals series privilege instead longer episodes comprising dozens of panels and tend to gravitate around genres delivered through long-form narration such as Fantasy, Romance and Drama.

3.4 Measures of Engagement

The following sections assess reader engagement with the 825 WEBTOON
Originals titles through a combination of publicly available measures of
readership, appreciation and fidelity, in the awareness that such quantitative
data can provide at best a proxy for reader engagement. The figures
examined below cannot be taken to reflect in full what a complex and
multifaceted reading experience is, which requires more qualitative
approaches such as those pioneered by the Reading Experience Database
(UK RED) and the READ-IT projects (Benatti et al. 2023; Crone and
Halsey 2012). They can, however, provide indications for further analysis.

3.4.1 Page Views

Page views represent an obvious proxy of reader engagement. Further
considerations are, however, necessary to qualify its apparent simplicity
before analysis and interpretation. The Page views numbers available
through web scraping do not measure the length or depth of readers'
interactions, which could range from an accidental hit lasting only seconds
to lengthy and deliberate close reading lasting several minutes. It is also not
possible to distinguish the repeat visits of an engaged reader from casual
one-off browsing or automated hits by internet bots. These additional
lenses are undoubtedly available to the editors at WEBTOON and are
most likely employed in the management and promotion of series. Even
simple page views are nonetheless a useful first port of call to identify the
most read series, which range in popularity from the staggering one billion
page views of *Lore Olympus*, *unOrdinary* and *Tower of God* to more modest
but still notable totals in the low hundreds of thousands. Overall,
WEBTOON Originals comics have accrued a remarkable 33 billion page
views between WEBTOON's debut on the English-language market in
2014 and the date of data acquisition in the third quarter of 2022, as shown in
Table 3. The actual total is likely to be even higher than the 33,107,087,944
calculated from the scraped data, due to WEBTOON's practice of rounding
numbers over one million to the nearest one hundred thousand.

It is worth noting that, of the 825 Originals series, 742 have achieved
one million views or more, 379 have accrued over 10 million views and only

Table 3. WEBTOON Originals page views grouped by Genre.

Genre	Sum of page views	Percentage of page views
Romance	8,959,223,258	27.1 percent
Fantasy	5,010,015,987	15.1 percent
Action	3,617,560,513	10.9 percent
Slice of Life	3,340,858,414	10.1 percent
Comedy	3,142,139,428	9.5 percent
Drama	2,821,487,709	8.5 percent
Superhero	1,332,231,716	4.0 percent
Thriller	1,329,611,562	4.0 percent
Supernatural	1,167,050,251	3.5 percent
Sci-fi	761,043,257	2.3 percent
Sports	747,297,038	2.3 percent
Horror	547,156,527	1.7 percent
Mystery	207,242,348	0.6 percent
Informative	75,069,936	0.2 percent
Historical	39,600,000	0.1 percent
Heartwarming	9,500,000	0.0 percent
Grand Total	33,107,087,944	100.00 percent

76 more than 100 million views. Just over 9 percent of the published series account therefore for 66 percent of the total WEBTOON Originals views, or almost 22 billion views in total. The remaining 90 percent of less popular series form a long tail that is responsible for just over one third of the total views. Only 16 series have accrued more than 400 million page views, with an additional 19 reaching between 200 and 400 million views and a further 39 series in the 100–200 million bracket.

Of the 16 Genres ascribed by WEBTOON to series, Romance and Fantasy account for the majority of page views, as shown in Table 3. Romance comics in particular are responsible for over one quarter (27.1 percent) of the total page views, followed by Fantasy with 15.1 percent. These two genres account for over 42.2 percent of total page views, with the following four genres (Action, Slice of Life, Comedy and Drama) comprising a further 39 percent of total page views. The remaining 10 genres add up to less than 20 percent of total page views, seeming to play a more marginal role on the platform.

3.4.2 Likes

In total, the 825 Originals series have received over 2.5 billion Likes (2,536,089,996). While the number of heart-shaped 'like' icons represents a crude measure of popularity, they are nonetheless symptomatic of a deeper reader engagement than simple page views. On WEBTOON, only readers who have registered for an account and are logged into it at the moment of reading can post a Like through a button located at the end of each episode. Each Like can therefore be considered as an act of voluntary communication, however brief, from the reader towards the publishers and authors.

WEBTOON Originals series range widely in the number of total Likes, from the over 50 million likes each of *My Giant Nerd Boyfriend*, *Lore Olympus*, *unOrdinary* and *Tower of God*, to more modest totals in the tens of thousands for less popular titles.

Of the 16 genres, Romance and Fantasy account for the majority of Likes, with Romance series in particular eliciting one quarter of the total Likes (25.8 percent), followed by Fantasy with 16.3 percent, as shown in Table 4.

3.4.3 Subscribers

The third measure of reader engagement is subscriptions. By subscribing to a series, readers receive instant notification of any new updates through their account in the mobile or web browser app. As is the case with Likes, subscription requires the reader to be logged into their WEBTOON account and to click a dedicated button, which is located on the homepage of each comics series. Subscription is not necessary for the fruition of comics, with readers being able to simply visit the series' page to discover new episodes or to use a search box. The choice to subscribe therefore represents an even deeper engagement with a comic and indicates a continuous interest that extends over time.

Table 4. WEBTOON Originals Likes grouped by Genre.

Genre	Total Likes	Percentage of total Likes
Romance	654,749,981	25.8 percent
Fantasy	412,161,443	16.3 percent
Slice of Life	271,882,519	10.7 percent
Drama	247,928,005	9.8 percent
Comedy	247,218,732	9.7 percent
Action	241,258,461	9.5 percent
Thriller	105,815,392	4.2 percent
Supernatural	94,360,739	3.7 percent
Superhero	70,632,023	2.8 percent
Sci-fi	67,095,413	2.6 percent
Sports	43,241,683	1.7 percent
Horror	41,910,358	1.7 percent
Mystery	24,678,360	1.0 percent
Historical	5,260,785	0.2 percent
Informative	4,696,102	0.2 percent
Heartwarming	3,200,000	0.1 percent
Grand Total	2,536,089,996	100.0 percent

As is the case with Page views and Likes, Romance and Fantasy are the genres that attract most Subscribers, as shown in Table 5.

The dominance of Romance (28.8 percent) and Fantasy (17.8 percent) is even more pronounced in the distribution of Subscribers, where they comprise almost half of the total, though within a context of diminishing scales. While views and likes are numbered in the billions, subscribers remain in the hundreds of millions. These figures nonetheless suggest a high level of baseline, repeated engagements with WEBTOON Original comics.

3.4.4 Ratings
By contrast with the extreme variations seen in Views, Likes and Subscribers, the average Ratings do not differ as markedly between Genres, as shown in

Table 5. WEBTOON Originals Subscribers grouped by Genre.

Genre	Total Subscribers	Percentage of total Subscribers
Romance	107,562,326	28.8 percent
Fantasy	66,599,893	17.8 percent
Action	38,479,814	10.3 percent
Drama	35,686,656	9.6 percent
Thriller	23,379,655	6.3 percent
Comedy	22,383,775	6.0 percent
Supernatural	19,888,094	5.3 percent
Slice of Life	16,630,561	4.5 percent
Sci-fi	10,464,201	2.8 percent
Superhero	10,194,315	2.7 percent
Horror	9,032,060	2.4 percent
Sports	6,243,511	1.7 percent
Mystery	3,797,206	1.0 percent
Historical	1,369,836	0.4 percent
Informative	1,274,183	0.3 percent
Heartwarming	477,822	0.1 percent
Grand Total	373,463,908	100.0 percent

Table 6. Unlike the three previous measures, the Genre with the highest average Ratings is Heartwarming, followed by Historical and then Fantasy. Romance occupies only the 10th position out of 16 genres.

This greater uniformity renders this measure of engagement a complex one to use. The WEBTOON Originals interface also does not display the number of readers who elect to leave ratings for each comic. As in the case of Likes and Subscriptions, only readers who are logged into their accounts can post a Rating.

3.5 Genres in WEBTOON Originals

Irrespective of the proxy measure employed, Romance and Fantasy emerge as the dominant genres in terms of metrics of reader engagement, followed

Table 6. WEBTOON Originals average Ratings grouped by genre.

Genre	Average Rating
Heartwarming	9.69
Historical	9.54
Fantasy	9.50
Mystery	9.48
Drama	9.45
Thriller	9.42
Horror	9.41
Supernatural	9.41
Action	9.40
Romance	9.37
Sci-fi	9.36
Sports	9.25
Slice of Life	9.24
Comedy	9.19
Informative	9.11
Superhero	8.86
Average	9.37

by a combination of Action, Drama, Comedy and Slice of Life. Superhero, the foremost genre of US print periodical comics, appears usually around the middle of the rankings. In addition, any analysis of the performance of the Superhero genre in WEBTOON must be qualified with the consideration that most of its engagement comes from one single series, *unOrdinary*, which is responsible for the almost totality of this genre's Views, Likes and Subscribers. In this context, the genre labelling of the four comics published in WEBTOON by DC Comics since 2021 is illuminating. Only one of them, *Vixen: NYC* (2022–23), is classified as Superhero, while the other three, *Zatanna and the Ripper*, *Red Hood: Outlaws* (both 2022–23) and

Eisner-nominated *Batman: Wayne Family Adventures* (2021–present), are billed as Fantasy, Action and Slice of Life, respectively. Even if they feature characters from one of the main superhero universes, such as Batman and Superman, the genre labels seem to direct readers' attention towards other elements of the comics, such as the interactions between Batman and the young superheroes who form his extended family. While this could be due to DC's attempt to differentiate its offerings, it nonetheless suggests an awareness that genres other than the Superhero seem to enjoy greater success on WEBTOON Originals.

The dominance of Romance and Fantasy within WEBTOON Originals is evident both in terms of numbers of series and in the size and attitude of their readerships. Together the two genres represent over 40 percent of the total page views, likes and subscriptions for the entire WEBTOON Originals platform. This preponderance will come as no surprise to readers familiar with the book market, where these forms of genre fiction dominate sales charts and are the main beneficiaries of the 'indie publishing' boom (Skains 2019 p. 31), especially for authors that begin their career on digital platforms such as Wattpad. WEBTOON's impact on the webcomics world lies similarly in providing a tangible demonstration to the English-language market that economic viability is possible when making these genres central to its offerings. Indeed, the rate by which Romance and Fantasy outstrip all other genres suggests that this differentiation from the practices of English-language comics publishers plays a central role in its success.

One explanation for this achievement could be located in WEBTOON's appeal to a different reader demographics than mainstream US publishers. In the book market, Romance and Fantasy tend to attract mostly female audience, who have been shown to constitute the majority of fiction readers (Taylor 2019 pp. 3–4). By offering an ample selection of titles in these genres, WEBTOON Originals are reaching out to an audience that, from the 1970s, was deemed of secondary importance by English-language publishers. Before the advent of the direct market distribution system, female readers were, by contrast, the bedrock of the more diverse genre offerings within US comics publishing (Robbins 2013 p. 118). As discussed in Sections 2.1 and 2.2, a young female audience found content that addressed their interests and priorities in the first place through the translation of manga (Erik-Soussi 2015 p. 36). Manga, until recently, remained chiefly a print medium, relying on physical distribution networks to reach its audience, albeit through widespread bookshops instead of more esoteric comics stores. Because of their book format, English-language manga have both a relatively high purchase cost (between $6.99 and $19.99 per volume) and a relatively infrequent publication schedule, usually monthly. In recent years, print manga have also been subjected to the limitations imposed by the Covid pandemic, which limited access to book-stores, and by shortages in the availability of paper, which have impacted the whole publishing industry. The rise in platforms that sell digital copies of manga and of subscription services can be located within these external circumstances, with 'digital first, digital only, subscription, and mobile apps' catering for a growing number of customers (Aoki 2022 p. 21). Digital manga have a lower purchase price (usually between $5.99–7.99) but still require a significant monetary outlay to read an entire series to conclusion, especially for a young public. Subscription models for digitised comics, such as ComiXology Unlimited or Crunchyroll Megafan, the latter of which also includes access to streaming anime series, represent a growing alternative to purchasing for perpetual ownership. Platforms for webtoons such as WEBTOON and Tapas/Kakao must therefore be contextualised within these shifts in the popularity of digitised comics, as well as being differentiated by their sales and monetisation models.

3.6 Author Gender in the 80 'Most Liked' WEBTOON Originals

As well as publishing comics that address the tastes of a predominantly female audience, WEBTOON Originals is also opening paths that can lead to professional comics careers for new authors (see Section 2.3.2). To assess whether these creators comprise more female and nonbinary authors that is still common in US print comics, the remainder of this section analyses in greater depth the 80 most read series as measured by the number of Likes. While aggregate values are discussed below, the full spreadsheet is available in the Supplementary Material and from the author upon request.

The number of comics was chosen to maintain comparability between the figures obtained from WEBTOON Originals and Tim Hanley's

'Women in Comics' statistics, which are based on the published output of DC and Marvel, as mentioned in Section 2.1 (2019a, 2019b, 2020b, 2020b). The two US publishers released a variable number of monthly comics in the period surveyed by Hanley (2016–20), with an average of 75-80 titles a month for each publisher. Perfect comparability is made impossible by the different publication models of print and webcomics. As discussed previously, print comics are released monthly, and webcomics are releasd weekly, or even more often. The DC and Marvel data covers a span of almost 5 years, while WEBTOON's is a snapshot of a particular moment in 2022. The inclusion of completed series can still help to provide a comparable perspective that extends beyond the current moment and shows longer-range trends for the period 2014–2022, when the WEBTOON English-language portal has been in operation. Hanley's figures are a very partial proxy for the US comics industries, but they nonetheless provide a benchmark, together with Woo's survey (Woo 2021).

3.6.1 The Derived Dataset

Tim Hanley's articles calculated initially (2016–19) the monthly percentage of female and nonbinary DC and Marvel authors over the overall number of authors for that month, and subsequently (2019–20) the percentage of monthly DC and Marvel comics with at least one female or nonbinary author. Both figures are therefore shown for the 80 most liked WEBTOON Originals series that are not translations of Korean webtoons.

After excluding from the dataset those comics that were translated from WEBTOON's Korean platform, which comprise 51 percent of the WEBTOON Originals titles (see Section 2.3), the top 80 WEBTOON Originals series as ranked by number of Likes were extracted into a derived dataset. These comprised a total of 93 named authors. It must be noted that numerous webtoons credit further 'helpers' or 'assistants', usually at the end of each instalment. However, these further names are usually not billed as equal authors in each series' masthead. An additional technical difficulty that militates against collecting these names is presented by their being published within the image files that constitute the body of the comic. Besides requiring further processing for machine readability, such as Optical Character Recognition, such image files could fall within the remit of the content that is protected by the author and publisher's copyright and intellectual property. This study is therefore focused on the gender of the authors listed for each comic in the WEBTOON Originals homepage (WEBTOON n.d.-a).

Together, the top 80 WEBTOON Originals comics, as measured by Likes, are responsible for over 15 billion page views, 1.1 billion likes and 114 million subscriptions. They account therefore for almost half of the total WEBTOON Originals page views and likes and for almost one third of its subscriptions, despite comprising just under 10 percent of the 825 WEBTOON Original series published by 2022. As mentioned, a distinction must be drawn between measures such as page views for webcomics and unit sales for print comics. As discussed in Section 3.1, US comics sales figures are for each monthly issue, whereas WEBTOON Originals page views and likes are cumulative over years. The 33 billion page views achieved by 825 WEBTOON Originals comics over 8 years may appear less remarkable when examined in this context. However, when it is remembered that the majority of these titles are by newcomers to the English-language market, the noteworthiness of their achievement is again increased. A more in-depth analysis of their authorship profiles can help to contextualise their achievements.

3.6.2 Analysis of Author and Editor Gender in WEBTOON Originals

For the top 80 comics ranked by the number of Likes, author gender was collected manually from publicly available sources. These included authors' profiles on WEBTOON, their social media accounts and online videos and interviews, as identified through links shared on the author's WEBTOON profile and through Google searches. Where these proved insufficient, fan-created data such as wiki pages on fandom.com or posts on publicly searchable discussion boards such as Reddit were included. No sources that required a login were included in the examination.

The categories employed for classification are female, male, nonbinary, and unknown for cases where information was unavailable and are shared in Table 7 as aggregates. Gender identity is, of course, far more complex and multifaceted than it is possible to portray in this study. Any classification, by necessity, flattens and simplifies diversity, disregarding nuances that may be of crucial importance to individuals and communities. With this underlying awareness, every effort was made to base genre classification on each individual author's assertions, with the goal of respecting their right to self-expression.

The 80 WEBTOON Original comics, as measured by Likes, were created by a total of 93 distinct authors. Of those, 62 authors, or 66 percent, sign their comics with pseudonyms, while 32 authors, or 34 percent, employ their actual name. It is worth noticing that some authors, such as instant-miso, Merryweather and Teo, appear on more than one comic (two for instantmiso, three for Merryweather and two for Teo). A total of 76 distinct authors are listed as first or sole creators, while a further 13 appear as second authors. A total of 4 authors are listed as third or subsequent authors, all coming from a single comic, *Batman: Wayne Family Adventures*. The order in which authors are listed may reflect an internal hierarchy. For example, Merryweather, who is identified as the head of Merryweather Media (Merryweather Media n.d.), appears as the first author with three different second authors. It may, however, be the result of other considerations. The two authors of *Purple Hyacinth*, Ephemeris and Sophism, are listed in each issue of their webtoon as responsible, respectively, for story (Ephemeris) and for story, art and soundtrack (Sophism). Yet despite Sophism's apparently larger contribution, she is listed second in the comics masthead. In comics that are adapted from other media, such as novels and webnovels, the author of the novel that is being adapted is often listed as the first author, such as Rebecca Schaeffer in *Not Even Bones* or Renée Ahdieh in *The Wrath and the Dawn*, but in other cases, they appear after other authors.

The gender classification of these 93 authors shows that a clear majority (65.6 percent) identify as female, as seen in Table 7. Another 20 percent identify as male, 5.4 percent as nonbinary, while for a further 8.6 percent, the author's gender cannot be determined from the information available on public sources.

Webtoons, as is the case with most comics, are often the product of multiple authors' labour (see Section 1.2), so it is beneficial to assess the gender composition of an entire creative team. Out of the 80 analysed

Table 7. Author gender of Top 80 English-language
WEBTOON Originals

Gender	Count of gender	Percent of gender
Female	61	65.6 percent
Male	19	20.4 percent
Nonbinary	5	5.4 percent
Unknown	8	8.6 percent
Grand Total	93	100.0 percent

creative teams, 55 (68.8 percent) contain at least one female author and 4 (5 percent) feature at least one author that identifies as nonbinary. In contrast with US periodical comics, only 14 out of the top 80 WEBTOON Originals creative teams (17.5 percent) have solely male authors, while for an additional 7 teams (8.8 percent), no author gender can be ascertained. This means that 59 out of 80 comics, or 73.8 percent, comprise at least one author who identifies as female or nonbinary. This percentage is more than double that found by Hanley in DC and Marvel comics published between 2019 and 2020 (2019b, 2020a, 2020b).

As noted in Section 2.1, Hanley's studies include editors and sub-editors in the list of authors. If the same methodology is applied, a further 14 authors are added, of whom 7 are female, 5 are male and 2 are of unknown gender. The number of WEBTOON Originals comics with at least one female or nonbinary author or editor therefore rises to 62 out of 80 comics, or 77.5 percent. This simple quantification appears to support the contention that WEBTOON Originals as a publisher is more receptive to female and nonbinary authors and more likely to offer them publishing opportunities than US print comics.

This statement can be further qualified through an assessment of the genre these female and nonbinary authors publish in, and of their measures of reader engagement. If only first authors are considered, female authors tend to concentrate in the Romance (20 comics by 19 authors) and Fantasy (8 comics) genres, with a spread of eight further genres, as shown in

Table 8. Female and nonbinary authors are not confined to specific genres and enjoy noticeable popularity with readers. In the 20 most liked WEBTOON Originals comics, the visibility of female and nonbinary authors is even more pronounced. Examples include the abovementioned fishball's *My Giant Nerd Boyfriend* (Slice of Life), Rachel Smythe's *Lore Olympus* (Romance), uru-chan's *unOrdinary* (Superhero), Leanne Krecic's *Let's Play* (Romance), Quimchee's *I Love Yoo* (Drama), Color_LES's *Mage and Demon Queen* (Comedy), Emma Krogell's *LUMINE* (Fantasy) and Wendy Lian Martin's *Castle Swimmer* (Fantasy).

Male authors, by contrast, seem to prefer working in the Comedy (8 comics by 7 authors) and Slice of Life genres (4 authors). Only a further 5 genres are represented, which surprisingly do not include Superhero. Romance and Fantasy are embraced by only one male first author each (see Table 9).

The small number of nonbinary first authors are split quite evenly between Slice of Life, Supernatural, Action and Sci-fi comics (see Table 10).

3.7 Evaluation

These data suggest that authors who publish on WEBTOON Originals and encounter above-average success there tend to be predominantly female. Even in cases where the first author of a webtoon identifies as male, authors or editors that identify as female or nonbinary are present in over three quarters of creative teams. In terms of genre, female-declaring authors tend to concentrate on the Romance and Fantasy genres, which are also those that attract the highest number of titles and over 40 percent of all Page views, Likes and Subscriptions. Female-identifying authors do not disdain humour-oriented genres such as Slice of Life and Comedy, which instead appear to be the main focus for authors declaring a male gender identity. As these last two genres tend to privilege short, episodic comics, female authors seem to prefer long-form serial comics, though exceptions do exist, such as the WEBTOON Originals with the highest number of Likes (over 60 million), *My Giant Nerd Boyfriend* by female creator fishball. The nonbinary authors included in the dataset embrace multiple genres.

Table 8. Genres chosen by female first authors in the Top 80 WEBTOON Originals comics.

Genre of comics with female first author	Count of Genre
Romance	20
Fantasy	8
Slice of Life	7
Drama	5
Supernatural	4
Comedy	3
Thriller	1
Mystery	1
Superhero	1
Sci-fi	1
Grand Total	51

Table 9. Genres chosen by male first authors in the Top 80 WEBTOON Originals comics.

Genre of comics by male first authors	Count of Genre
Comedy	8
Slice of Life	4
Sci-fi	2
Drama	1
Supernatural	1
Fantasy	1
Romance	1
Grand Total	18

The gender distribution of the top WEBTOON authors reflects the tastes and probably the composition of its audience, which is unsurprising given the reliance of the publisher on participatory culture mechanisms, as embedded

Table 10. Genres chosen by nonbinary
first authors.

Genre	Count of Genre
Slice of Life	2
Supernatural	1
Action	1
Sci-fi	1
Grand Total	5

within the Canvas platform (see Section 2.4). The user-generated content surfaced through competition crowdsourcing is used by WEBTOON to promote those comics that are most appreciated by its audience. The findings of this study that about 70 percent of the most successful WEBTOON Originals authors identify as female or nonbinary seem to correlate with WEBTOON's own assessment of its audience, which it describes as comprised of 'around 60 percent' female users (WEBTOON 2023a). Such crowdsourced pipeline was, for example, at the origin of two of the most successful WEBTOON Originals series. Rachel Smythe's *Lore Olympus* was originally self-published on Canvas, while uru-chan's *unOrdinary* was discovered through a 'a superhero contest' (Griepp 2019). Both of these successful creators are female and both are first-time comics authors, without a prior history of publication. It is doubtful whether conventional comics publishers would have included them given their lack of a track record, though WEBTOON's trust in their works has been more than repaid by the billions of page views, printed book sales and publicity they have since generated.

The data collected through webscraping shows that WEBTOON is succeeding in exploiting the new space first created in the English-language comics market by innovative webcomics, periodicals and manga authors. It is accomplishing this task by publishing comics in genres, such as Romance and Fantasy that provide publication and visibility for author demographics still perceived as secondary within English-language print comics. Whether these opportunities translate into full-time creative careers for these authors remains an open question, which the next and conclusive section will address.

4 Conclusions, Next Steps, Bibliography

This study has shown that webcomics, especially those in the webtoon vertical format, are revolutionising the comics medium from the perspective of both format and publishing circuits. As webcomics represent 'the comics vanguard' (Misemer 2021 p. 221), the activities of authors and readers on the largest webcomics platform, WEBTOON, deserve to be studied as they point towards notable developments for the medium. Attention should be focused, in particular, on three aspects.

4.1 The WEBTOON Innovations

4.1.1 Innovations in Format

The first innovation brought by webtoons is the breaking of the dependence of webcomics upon print paradigms (see Section 1). The creation of the webtoon vertical scrolling layout has established the first born-digital comics format that is not reliant on the adaptation of print. As well as realising to an extent the aspirations of the 'infinite canvas' (McCloud 2009), the continuous vertical scroll of webtoons is exploiting digital publication frameworks that target the small screens of the most ubiquitous mobile devices (see Section 1.5). Mobile webtoon platforms integrate infrastructures for the consumption, reception, distribution and sale of webcomics within a single interface. Instead of a geographically dispersed circuit where physical comics must be printed in one location, distributed to points of sale, purchased by readers and carried to where they will be consumed, most of the phases of Darnton's communications circuit are collapsed within readers' digital devices. This has enabled webcomics and webtoons in particular to sidestep the restrictions imposed by external events such as the Covid-19 pandemic (see Section 1.2), and to reach a truly global audience.

4.1.2 Innovations in Genre

In addition to these significant formal and infrastructural innovations, the second advance of webtoons regards the broadening of comics genres (see Section 3). The results of this study show that WEBTOON Originals is making a positive contribution to the expansion of genre diversity in comics publishing. These developments build upon and amplify trends that were begun by manga, other types of webcomics and a growing number of small- and medium-sized comics publishers such as Boom! Studios, IDW, Image and Dark Horse. Within WEBTOON Originals, titles such as *Lore Olympus*, *Let's Play*, *My Giant Nerd Boyfriend*, *Mage and Demon Queen*, *Castle Swimmer*, *Purple Hyacinth* and *Gourmet Hound* are broadening the genre range of mainstream English-language comics to include Romance, Fantasy, Drama, Comedy and Mystery, while titles such as *unOrdinary* expand the remit of the Superhero genre beyond consolidated universes such as DC's and Marvel's. Within WEBTOON, long-form comics in these and other genres have the option to flourish and to achieve visibility and commercial viability, as attested by the millions of readers who have left traces of their interactions through page views, likes and subscriptions.

4.1.3 Innovations in Authorship

The third webtoon revolution lies in the provision of structured pathways for the emergence of a range of new, more diverse authors into the comics medium (see Section 2 and 3). The participatory circuits of webtoons are enabling a growing number of female and nonbinary creators to transform from self-published 'produsers' to successful comics professionals (see Section 2.3) and to share their ideas with new communities (Galvan 2018 p. 433; Hatfield 2015 p. 65). The emergence of platforms such as WEBTOON into webcomics communication circuits has facilitated these new opportunities while at the same time introducing new complexities. On the one hand, their establishment can be seen as a sign of the growing maturity of the webcomics format and communications circuits. By developing the technologies behind mobile webtoon apps and devising monetisation strategies balanced between free and paid access, webtoon publishers are consolidating and promoting the format, which has now come firmly to the attention of mainstream media (see, for example, Davies and Song 2022; Gustines and Stevens 2022). On the other hand, though, the arrival of these players can be interpreted as a corporatisation or 'platformisation' (Kim and Yu 2019 p. 1) and a potential stifling of the webcomics medium. WEBTOON and other platforms such as Tapas/Kakao have positioned themselves as privileged intermediaries between authors and readers. The collaborative, parasocial dialogue between these agents identified in Section 1.4 is therefore mediated by the presence of the platforms, who pursue their own agendas, sometimes clashing with the perspectives of audiences and creators.

4.2 The WEBTOON Challenges

This last nexus of platformisation and authorship/readership needs to be scrutinised and evaluated carefully. Webtoon platforms exact an indirect but high price from authors and readers for the use of their infrastructures, in terms of both labour, attention and money, as is the case with other contemporary models of 'social' or 'demotic' authorship (Ramdarshan Bold 2018; Skains 2010).

In the specific instance of WEBTOON Originals, a number of authors have argued that the practices of the platform do not sufficiently recognise the labour of creators. In September 2022, WEBTOON authors, Chase Keels and Miranda Mundt (*LoveBot*, *Muted*), published an open letter, alleging a lack of transparency in the calculation and distribution of revenue arising from advertisements and Fast Pass (Mundt and Keels 2022). Particularly concerning, according to the authors, was WEBTOON's alleged tardiness in sharing reader engagement metrics with their creators. Since Fast Pass remuneration depends upon reader numbers, as measured through more granular versions of metrics such as those employed in Section 3, Mundt and Keels' accusation is particularly worrying for creators. Their complaints were echoed in a lively Twitter debate with other WEBTOON creators (Mundt 2022), which hinted at a deterioration of conditions and an unsustainable increase in workload for authors. Creator Emmet Hobbes further claimed a lack of marketing support from WEBTOON and poor communications, blaming these difficulties for the suspension of his series *Royale* after less than twenty episodes (Hobbes 2022). Mundt and Keels' open letter claimed that certain creators earn 'less than 300$ USD for each 40 panel episode', due to the need to pay for the assistants they require to meet their deadlines out of their weekly earnings (Mundt and Keels 2022). Furthermore, a short-lived Twitter account, called WebtoonExposed alleged a significant 'difference in pay for the Latin

America creators vs. US creators' (Tanski 2022b). According to this Twitter account, which has since been removed, authors signing contracts through the WEBTOON Latin America branch are subject to far lower remunerations than creators signing through the US branch. It is as yet unclear how WEBTOON is responding to these complaints.

The situation in webtoons is mirrored by the struggles of comic creators and authors more generally. The remuneration of print comics professionals has seen little or no increase over the past decades, with page rates for writers, pencillers and inkers stagnating or even decreasing when adjusted for inflation, including '$75–100 per page' for writers and '$100–175 per page' for pencillers (Tanski 2022a). Incomes for writers in all genres have entered a downward spiral accelerated by the Covid-19 pandemic, which has seen median earnings for UK authors fall from '38.2% (in real terms) since the last survey in 2018 (i.e., from £11,329 to £7,000)' in 2021 (Thomas et al. 2022 p. 7). The remuneration rates offered by WEBTOON must be placed within this context to be fully appraised. If the rate reported by Mundt and Keels of $300 per weekly episode after paying assistants is correct, it would translate to $12,000 or £9,900 per year, assuming 40 weeks of comic production. This level of remuneration could be compared favourably with that of professional authors, but it must be counterbalanced by the unique demands of comics. In addition to their still limited recognition within literature or art, the position of WEBTOON Original creators is complicated by their placement in a liminal space between self-publishing amateurism in the platform economy and full-blown professionalisation. Working for WEBTOON can offer a more regular income than relying on crowdfunded donations from fans or on advertisement revenue. However, the demands placed on authors can be high, such as the intense workloads needed in order to comply with the weekly pace of serialisation.

The achievements of numerous WEBTOON Originals authors in sustaining weekly serials over several years should dispel any doubts about their abilities and commitment. A comparison with previous forms of serial media, such as Victorian novels, can help to place them in context. Victorian serial authors such as G.W.M. Reynolds published serial novels such as *The Mysteries of London* and its follow-up *The Mysteries of the Court of London* with consistently high sales during the period 1844–55, producing 'nearly half a million words' (James 2010 pp. 100–1). Even the most influential serial novelist, Charles Dickens, usually published his works in shorter bursts of 18 monthly numbers, with breaks between the end of one novel and the commencement of the next. WEBTOON Originals series such as *Lore Olympus* have been ongoing for more than 5 years, publishing thousands of panels in hundreds of weekly issues. In terms of serial publication, this is an achievement that is worthy of notice, especially as it comes from mostly novice authors striking out a career with little or no initial support. In US periodical comics, the longest run by a single author is considered to be Chris Claremont's 16-year authorship of *Uncanny X-Men* between 1975 and 1991. It remains a milestone in comics for the richness of its plots and characterisation, which the author was able to develop through hundreds of monthly issues and thousands of pages. Yet Claremont was not alone in his work but part of a team with artists such as John Byrne and Walter Simonson, who shared the burden of producing regular content. They were supported by a further team of editors, such as Louise Simonson, and by assistants who provided advice on content, as well as support for promotion and marketing. It is still the norm for US periodical comics to be attributed to at least two authors, writer and penciller, if not more, in an explicit acknowledgement of the collective effort needed to create regular serialised comics (see Section 1.3).

By contrast, the WEBTOON Originals authors often work with little support, especially at the beginning of their careers, when they are making an awkward transition from gifted amateurs to full-time professionals. That the process is not yet a smooth one is borne out by their continued recourse to crowdfunding platforms such as Patreon even while contracted to WEBTOON Originals. An analysis of the stated crowdfunding goals of several prominent WEBTOON authors reveals that, even successful creators such as Quimchee, whose webcomic *I Love Yoo* has accumulated over 500 million page views, require additional funds to create a support team (www.patreon.com/quimchee). Further examples include Color_LES, author of *Mage and Demon Queen* (over 320 million page views) and Junepurr, author of *Sub Zero* (over 330 million page views), all comics that are in the top 5 percent on WEBTOON Originals for page views and likes. Helpers such as colourists and line assistants are often mentioned among Patreon campaign goals, with frequently cited motivations including greater continuity of outputs and preserving the authors' mental and physical health. Health complications caused by overworking are indeed frequently stated as causes for hiatuses in scheduled WEBTOON Originals comics. WEBTOON seems to be aware of the strain its publishing models are imposing on creators, especially those who are invited to make the transition from self-published Canvas series to contracted WEBTOON Originals. Its public response, however, appears for the moment to be limited to the provision of wellbeing awareness resources rather than an open discussion of the implications of publishing within WEBTOON Originals.

Webtoon platforms such as WEBTOON and Tapas/Kakao are falling under increasing scrutiny in this regard in their native Korea, as demonstrated by their CEOs, Junkoo Kim and Jinsoo Lee, being questioned in the Korean National Assembly over employment practices (Yoon 2021). The increasing scrutiny accorded to creative industries and to webcomics in particular has resulted in the creation of standard employment contracts, though they are at present 'a recommendation, not a requirement' (Kim and Lee 2022 p. 8). Kakao's recent creation of a 10 billion won ($7.7 million) fund to help creators struggling with mental health and income difficulties (Yoon 2022b) can be read as a sign of its growing awareness of the need to cultivate its creators. Institutions in the English-language market have so far not monitored the operations of webcomics publishers at such high levels, but their success is likely to bring their business practices under greater scrutiny.

4.3 Potential Futures

What approaches can be envisaged to address these tensions? The power disproportion between giant platforms and individual creators paints at first sight a bleak picture. At the same time, approaches that include the platforms in the collaborative circuits between readers and authors may offer hope for the future.

Forms of organisation and collective bargaining are slowly emerging on other platforms, such as the formation of the YouTubers Union and its

FairTube campaign (Niebler 2020 pp. 223–7). These same platforms are providing increasing acknowledgement of creators as partners (Cunningham and Craig 2019 pp. 6–7). As a platform for cultural content, certain of WEBTOON's behaviours seem to indicate that it too regards creators as more than mere subordinates, implicitly recognising its dependence upon them for 'the continuous production of cultural commodities' (Kim and Yu 2019 p. 7). One possibility for the improvement of creator conditions within WEBTOON could be for more authors to be given the resources to develop into small business entrepreneurs. They could, over time, form and lead a studio composed of trained support professionals, such as colourists, inkers and letterers. Such a model is the norm in Japanese manga, and though fraught with opportunities for exploitation, it could be the most viable compromise between authorial freedom and reader (and publisher) demand for regular, consistent content. These creator-led small studios could strike a middle ground between the models of the sole genius and the top-down corporate structure typical of US superhero publishers. One example of this approach is Rachel Smythe, who has developed such a team to assist with the creation of *Lore Olympus,* as recognised in recent interviews (Graves 2022). Smythe recruited her assistants from the ranks of her readers and was enabled to support them through her income from WEBTOON, in turn facilitating the delivery of her series through over 200 weekly episodes. The success and viability of her approach seem to be confirmed by her achievement of three of the most prestigious prizes for webcomics in 2022, the Eisner, Harvey and Ringo Awards, and by the successful print publication of her work through Penguin Random House. As *Lore Olympus* ranks among the most successful WEBTOON Originals series, Smythe's trajectory presents a best-case scenario for creators.

If the comparison with Dickens is extended, the English author himself at first published his serial novels within established periodicals, such as *Bentley's Miscellany*, where he serialised *Oliver Twist*. Once he had become a household name, he was able to develop a format more suited to his talents, that of monthly parts released with his chosen publishers. Such a model enabled him to publish titles that succeeded in becoming milestones in British literature, such as *David Copperfield* and *Bleak House*, and to achieve remarkable incomes. Finally, Dickens established his own weekly periodicals, *Household Words* (1850–9) and *All the Year Round* (1859–70), where he published not only his own novels but also offered opportunities to other Victorian authors such as Wilkie Collins and Elizabeth Gaskell. Both eventually left Dickens's periodicals to strike out their own paths, but this apprenticeship within another writer's team provided them with essential expertise that they were able to employ in their later careers. Dickens was not faultless as a manager and editor, often being unwilling to relinquish control over the content of his periodicals. Nonetheless, he created publication formats that found success with readers and critics alike, transforming the world of Victorian publishing and providing readers with affordable venues for high-quality content. A WEBTOON Originals platform that enabled authors to similarly build and sustain their own studios could increase its transformative effect on English-language comics publishing and on authors' lives, especially if female or nonbinary, while ensuring the sustainability of series in the long run. It could be argued that the abrupt termination or suspension of successful comics through overworking and burnout is more costly to WEBTOON than increasing authors' starting remuneration. If their crowdfunding goals are to be believed, relatively modest increases to monthly incomes would suffice to grant authors a better quality of life and to ensure greater continuity and quality of content for publishers. An increased level of openness about the obligations and pressures of a professional webcomics career could also benefit both publishers and authors. Instead of the myth of the lone creator earning millions through a labour of love and creativity, the realities of deadlines, the constant need for self-promotion and the relationship with a demanding audience should be emphasised and openly discussed between established and aspiring authors, publishers, as well as the reading public. Initial goodwill towards the platform that gives new authors a voice runs the risk of dwindling away through exhaustion and disillusionment.

It is to be hoped that greater transparency in matters of contracts, remuneration and workload expectations will arise out of these debates, in turn leading to improved conditions for creators and more regular content for the platforms. This shift by authors and publishers towards greater dialogue can bring rich rewards for both, as shown through the earnings made public in regard to the Korean parent platform, Naver WEBTOON. For the English-language market, it is likely that the increasing consolidation and maturity of the webtoon platforms, their growing successes with audience and critics and the burgeoning transmedia connections between webtoons and other media can help more creators earn a sustainable living as webtoon authors. Such an outcome would in turn maximise the already positive effects of WEBTOON Originals on content and author diversity, as is manifested tangibly through its audience engagement metrics.

A final consideration regards the availability of these metrics for the future. As most engagement data are displayed publicly on the WEBTOON site, audience metrics can be openly scrutinised by readers and researchers alike. However, this openness exposes WEBTOON's content to potential exploitation, for example, through unregulated scraping and ingestion for the training of AI tools such as large language models and image generation models. The recent change in Terms of Use that prohibits webscraping can be interpreted as part of an attempt to protect the viability of the platform and therefore also of authors' careers. At the same time, the increased prominence of WEBTOON series makes them an essential part of any study of contemporary webcomics and their audiences, for which large-scale data collection plays an essential role. The centrality of readers in the webcomics communication circuit, for example, deserves to be the focus of the next phase of research on webcomics. After quantifying the recent innovations in comics genre and author gender, the motivations and outcomes of reading experiences should be investigated to better understand why readers choose to read webcomics, to become involved in this participatory and platformised communications circuit, or to make the step from reader to creator. Access to data from webtoon platforms, acquired in collaboration with publishers, is going to be crucial for such an endeavour. It is to be hoped that through mutual engagement, platforms, creators and researchers will be able to find approaches that can enable the study of webtoons in detail and at scale, while protecting livelihoods and creativity.

References

Aggleton, J (2019) Defining Digital Comics: A British Library Perspective. *Journal of Graphic Novels and Comics*, 10(4), 393–409. https://doi.org/10.1080/21504857.2018.1503189.

Allen, T (2014) *Economics of Digital Comics*, Indignant Media.

Alverson, B (2017, October 19) NYCC Insider Sessions Powered by ICv2: A Demographic Snapshot of Comics Buyers. Retrieved 9 November 2021, from https://icv2.com/articles/news/view/38709/nycc-insider-sessions-powered-icv2-a-demographic-snapshot-comics-buyers.

Antonini, A, Brooker, S, and Benatti, F (2020) Circuits, Cycles, Configurations: An Interaction Model of Web Comics. In A.-G. Bosser, D. E. Millard, and C. Hargood, eds., *Interactive Storytelling*, Cham: Springer, 287–299. https://doi.org/10.1007/978-3-030-62516-0_26.

Antonini, A, Vignale, F, Gravier, G, and Ouvry-Vial, B (2019, July 17) The Model of Reading: Modelling principles, Definitions, Schema, Alignments., HAL. https://hal-univ-lemans.archives-ouvertes.fr/hal-02301611.

Aoki, D (2022) Manga Is Booming. *Publishers Weekly*, 269(19), 21. http://www.proquest.com/docview/2657518858/abstract/A88C4009F829404DPQ/24.

Batinić, J (2022a) Digital Comics. In E. La Cour, S. Grennan, and R. Spanjers, eds., *Key Terms in Comics Studies*, Cham (Switzerland): Palgrave Macmillan, 86.

Batinić, J (2022b) Webcomics. In E. La Cour, S. Grennan, and R. Spanjers, eds., *Key Terms in Comics Studies*, Cham (Switzerland): Palgrave Macmillan, 350.

Baudry, J (2018) Paradoxes of Innovation in French Digital Comics. *The Comics Grid: Journal of Comics Scholarship*, 8(4). https://doi.org/10.16995/cg.108.

Beat Staff (2022) Trans Comic Creators for Trans Day of Visibility (March 31). www.comicsbeat.com/31-trans-comic-creators-for-trans-day-of-visibility-march-31/ (accessed 12 June 2023).

Beetham, M (1990) Towards a Theory of the Periodical as a Publishing Genre. In L. Brake, A. Jones, and L. Madden, eds., *Investigating Victorian Journalism*, Houndmills: Macmillan Press, 19–32.

Benatti, F (2019) Superhero Comics and the Digital Communications Circuit: A Case Study of *Strong Female Protagonist*. *Journal of Graphic Novels and Comics*, 10(3), 306–319. https://doi.org/10.1080/21504857.2018.1485720.

Benatti, F, Vignale, F, Antonini, A, and King, E (2023) Reading in Europe – Challenges and Lessons Learned from the Case Studies of the READ-IT Project. *Digital Scholarship in the Humanities*, 38(2), 477–481. https://doi.org/10.1093/llc/fqac071.

Bolter, JD, and Grusin, RA (1996) Remediation. *Configurations*, 4(3), 311–358. https://doi.org/10.1353/con.1996.0018.

Brienza, C (2016) *Manga in America: Transnational Book Publishing and the Domestication of Japanese Comics*, Bloomsbury.

Burlew, R (2020) Rich Burlew Is Creating the Order of the Stick (and the GITP forums). Retrieved 16 September 2022, from www.patreon.com/oots.

Cabeal, D (2015, February 27) An Interview With JunKoo Kim Creator of LINE Webtoon. https://comicbastards.com/comics/an-interview-with-junkoo-kim-creator-of-line-webtoon.

Cain, S (2017, April 3) Marvel Executive Says Emphasis on Diversity May have Alienated Readers. *The Guardian*. www.theguardian.com/books/2017/apr/03/marvel-executive-says-emphasis-on-diversity-may-have-alienated-readers.

Campbell, T (2006) *A History of Webcomics*, San Antonio, TX: Antarctic Press. http://archive.org/details/historyofwebcomi0000camp.

Cavna, M (2012, February 21) New Kickstarter Record: 'Order of the Stick' Webcomic Creator Rich Burlew Cites 'Huge Geeky Safety Net' in $1.2M Donation Campaign. www.washingtonpost.com/blogs/comic-riffs/post/new-kickstarter-record-order-of-the-stick-webcomic-creator-rich-burlew-cites-huge-geeky-safety-net-in-12m-donation-campaign/2012/02/21/gIQAbMJSRR_blog.html.

Cedeira Serantes, L (2019) *Young People, Comics and Reading: Exploring a Complex Reading Experience*, Cambridge: Cambridge University Press. https://doi.org/10.1017/9781108568845.

Chartier, R (1995) *Forms and Meanings: Texts, Performances, and Audiences from Codex to Computer*, Philadelphia: University of Pennsylvania Press.

Cho, H (2016) The Webtoon: A New Form for Graphic Narrative. *The Comics Journal*. www.tcj.com/the-webtoon-a-new-form-for-graphic-narrative/.

Cho, H (2021) The Platformization of Culture: Webtoon Platforms and Media Ecology in Korea and Beyond. *The Journal of Asian Studies*, 80(1), 73–93. https://doi.org/10.1017/S0021911820002405.

Chute, HL (2010) *Graphic Women: Life Narrative and Contemporary Comics*, New York: Columbia University Press.

Cocca, C (2016) *Superwomen: Gender, Power, and Representation*, New York: Bloomsbury Academic.

Comic Book Legal Defense Fund (2015) She Changed Comics – Comic Book Legal Defense Fund. https://cbldf.org/she-changed-comics/.

Comichron (2022) Comichron: April 2022 Comic Book Sales to Comics Shops. Retrieved 23 November 2022, from www.comichron.com/monthlycomicssales/2022/2022-04.html.

Crone, R, and Halsey, K (2012) On Collecting, Cataloguing and Collating the Evidence of Reading: The 'RED Movement' and Its Implications for Digital Scholarship. In T. Weller, ed., *History in the Digital Age*,

London: Routledge, 95–110. www.routledge.com/books/details/9780415666961/.

Cunningham, S, and Craig, D (2019) Creator Governance in Social Media Entertainment. *Social Media + Society*, 5(4), 205630511988342. https://doi.org/10.1177/2056305119883428.

Dahlan, HA (2022) The Publishing and Distribution System of Japanese Manga and Doujinshi. *Publishing Research Quarterly*, 653–64. https://doi.org/10.1007/s12109-022-09919-9.

Darnton, R (1982) What Is the History of Books? *Daedalus*, 111(3), 65–83. https://doi.org/10.2307/20024803.

Davies, C, and Song, J (2022, March 25) South Korea's Webtoon Companies Target Global Takeover. *Financial Times*. www.ft.com/content/e07dc473-cfcb-47be-b757-c4f4b63871f2.

Davis, L (2012, January 20) Ryan Estrada and Dorothy Gambrell Chart Their Income as Webcomic and Freelance Cartoonists. Retrieved 5 September 2022, from https://comicsalliance.com/income-chart-webcomics-cartoonist-gambrell-estrada/.

Donnelly, M (2019, July 23) Women Creators, Fans at Comic-Con Rise Up Against Culture of Misogyny. https://variety.com/2019/film/features/women-at-comic-con-fan-culture-1203276161/.

Dowthwaite, L (2017, September) *Crowdfunding Webcomics* (PhD), Nottingham: University of Nottingham. https://eprints.nottingham.ac.uk/50969/1/Liz%20Dowthwaite%20Thesis%20-%20Final%20revised%20version.pdf.

Duffy, BE, Poell, T, and Nieborg, DB (2019) Platform Practices in the Cultural Industries: Creativity, Labor, and Citizenship. *Social Media + Society*, 5(4), 205630511987967. https://doi.org/10.1177/2056305119879672.

Erik-Soussi, M (2015) The Western Sailor Moon Generation: North American Women and Feminine-friendly Global Manga. In

C. Brienza, ed., *Global Manga: "Japanese" Comics without Japan?*, Farnham: Ashgate, 23–44.

European Parliament (2016, April 27) Regulation (EU) 2016/679 of the European Parliament and of the Council of 27 April 2016 on the Protection of Natural Persons with Regard to the Processing of Personal Data and on the Free Movement of Such Data, and Repealing Directive 95/46/EC (General Data Protection Regulation). Retrieved 23 November 2022, from https://eur-lex.europa.eu/eli/reg/2016/679.

Fenty, S, Houp, T, and Taylor, L (2004) Webcomics: The Influence and Continuation of the Comix Revolution. *ImageTexT: Interdisciplinary Comics Studies*, 1(2). www.english.ufl.edu/imagetext/archives/v1_2/group/index.shtml.

Findlay, B (2010) Subscription Publishing. In Suarez MF and Woudhuysen HR, eds., *The Oxford Companion to the Book*, Oxford: Oxford University Press. www.oxfordreference.com/view/10.1093/acref/9780198606536.001.0001/acref-9780198606536-e-4727.

Galvan, M (2018) 'The Lesbian Norman Rockwell': Alison Bechdel and Queer Grassroots Networks. *American Literature*, 90(2), 407–438. https://doi.org/10.1215/00029831-4564358.

Galvan, M, and Misemer, L (2019) Introduction: The Counterpublics of Underground Comics. *Inks (Columbus, Ohio: 2017)*, 3(1), 1–5. https://doi.org/10.1353/ink.2019.0000.

Gambrell, D (2017, June 17) Cash Money 2016. Retrieved 26 September 2022, from https://web.archive.org/web/20170617015526/http://catandgirl.com/cash-money-2010/.

Garrity, S (2011) The History of Webcomics. *The Comics Journal*. www.tcj.com/the-history-of-webcomics/.

Garrity, S (2013) One of Those Things. *The Comics Journal*. www.tcj.com/one-of-those-things/.

Goldhaber, MH (1997) The Attention Economy and the Net. *First Monday*, 2(4). https://doi.org/10.5210/fm.v2i4.519.

Goodbrey, DM (n.d.) E-merl.com ~ New Experiments In Fiction. Retrieved 20 April 2017, from http://e-merl.com/.

Gordon, I (2013) Comics, Creators, and Copyright: On the Ownership of Serial Narratives by Multiple Authors. In J. Gray and D. Johnson, eds., *A Companion to Media Authorship*, Oxford: Wiley-Blackwell, 221–236. https://doi.org/10.1002/9781118505526.ch11.

Graves, S (2022, August 8) Eisner Winner Rachel Smythe on the *Lore Olympus* Season 2 Finale. Retrieved 9 August 2022, from https://gizmodo.com/rachel-smythe-lore-olympus-hades-persephone-webtoon-1849379157.

Griepp, M (2019, September 6) Webtoon Comics Platform Running Multi-Million Dollar Ad Campaign on TV, Web, in Theaters, and Outdoor. Retrieved 10 November 2021, from https://icv2.com/articles/news/view/43985/webtoon-comics-platform-running-multi-million-dollar-ad-campaign-tv-web-theaters-outdoor.

Griepp, M (2022, June 30) Comics and Graphic Novel Sales Grew Over 60% in 2021. Retrieved 2 August 2022, from https://icv2.com/articles/markets/view/51531/comics-graphic-novel-sales-grew-over-60-2021?utm_source=dlvr.it&utm_medium=twitter.

Groensteen, T (2007) *The System of Comics*, Jackson: University Press of Mississippi.

Gustines, GG, and Stevens, M (2022, July 23) Comics That Read Top to Bottom Are Bringing in New Readers. *The New York Times*. www.nytimes.com/2022/07/23/arts/digital-comics-new-readers.html.

Hanley, T (2019a, February 15) Women in Comics, By The Numbers: Summer and Fall 2018. www.comicsbeat.com/women-in-comics-by-the-numbers-summer-and-fall-2018/.

Hanley, T (2019b, May 16) Women in Comics, By The Numbers: Winter 2019. www.comicsbeat.com/women-in-comics-numbers-winter-2019/.

Hanley, T (2020a, September 29) Women & NB Creators at DC Comics, October 2020 Solicits – 22 Creators on 17 Books. https://thanley.word press.com/2020/09/29/women-nb-creators-at-dc-comics-october-2020-solicits-22-creators-on-17-books/.

Hanley, T (2020b, September 30) Women & NB Creators at Marvel Comics, October 2020 Solicits – 17 Creators on 16 Books. https:// thanley.wordpress.com/2020/09/30/women-nb-creators-at-marvel-comics-october-2020-solicits-17-creators-on-16-books/.

Hatfield, NK (2015) TRANSforming Spaces: Transgender Webcomics as a Model for Transgender Empowerment and Representation within Library and Archive Spaces. *Queer Cats Journal of LGBTQ Studies*, 1(1), 57–73. http://escholarship.org/uc/item/3g15q00g.pdf.

Hawkins, M, Cheung, J, and Šejić, L (2018) *Swing*, Vol. 1, Los Angeles: Top Cow Productions.

Hayles, NK (2008) *Electronic Literature: New Horizons for the Literary*, Notre Dame: University of Notre Dame.

Helmond, A (2015) The Platformization of the Web: Making Web Data Platform Ready. *Social Media + Society*, 1(2), 205630511560308. https:// doi.org/10.1177/2056305115603080.

Hobbes, E (2022, September 8) Reply to Miranda Mundt's open letter. *Twitter*, Tweet. https://twitter.com/EmmettComix/status/1567980833 138671616.

Horton, D, and Wohl, RR (1956) Mass Communication and Para-Social Interaction: Observations on Intimacy at a Distance. *Psychiatry*, 19(3), 215–229. www.participations.org/volume%203/issue%201/3_01_hor tonwohl.htm.

Hou J, Rashid J and Lee K M (2017) Cognitive map or medium materiality? Reading on paper and screen. *Computers in Human Behavior*, 67, 84–94. https://doi.org/10.1016/j.chb.2016.10.014.

Ivy Plus Libraries Confederation (n.d.) Global Webcomics. Retrieved 24 May 2023, from https://archive-it.org/collections/10181.

jackson, remus, and Stewart-Taylor, F (2020) Reading Trans Autobiographical Comics through Trans Phenomenology. Retrieved 11 June 2023, from www.internationalcomicartsforum.org/1/post/2020/11/reading-trans-autobiographical-comics-through-trans-phenomenology.html.

James, L (2010) From Egan To Reynolds: The Shaping of Urban 'Mysteries' in England and France, 1821–48. *European Journal of English Studies*, 14(2), 95–106. https://doi.org/10.1080/13825571003775356.

Jenkins, H (2006a) *Convergence Culture: Where Old and New Media Collide*, New York: NYU Press.

Jenkins, H (2006b) *Fans, Bloggers, and Gamers: Exploring Participatory Culture*, New York: New York University Press. http://ebookcentral.proquest.com/lib/open/detail.action?docID=865571.

Jin, DY (2015) Digital Convergence of Korea's Webtoons: Transmedia Storytelling. *Communication Research and Practice*, 1(3), 193–209. https://doi.org/10.1080/22041451.2015.1079150.

Johnson, S, and Garrick, D (1763) Prologue Spoken By Mr. Garrick, At the Opening of the Theatre in Drury-lane 1747. By the Same. In *A Collection Of Poems In Six Volumes*, London: J. Dodsley, 200–202. http://libezproxy.open.ac.uk/login? www.proquest.com/books/prologue-spoken-mr-garrick-at-opening-theatre/docview/2147678755/se-2?accountid=14697.

Kim, C, and Lee, S (2022) Putting Creative Labour in Its Place in the Shadow of the Korean Wave. *International Journal of Cultural Policy*, 29(5), 603–617. https://doi.org/10.1080/10286632.2022.2087643.

Kim, J-H (2023) Platform Economy and Gig Work in South Korea: A Special Focus on Naver and Kakao. In Ness I, ed., *The Routledge Hanbook of the Gig Economy*, Abingdon: Routledge, 419–432.

Kim, J-H, and Yu, J (2019) Platformizing Webtoons: The Impact on Creative and Digital Labor in South Korea. *Social Media + Society*, 5 (4), 1–11. https://doi.org/10.1177/2056305119880174.

Kim, R (2022) Webtoons: From Scrolling to Streaming. In Kim, R, ed., *Hallyu! The Korean Wave*, London: Victoria & Albert Museum, 72–81.

Kleefeld, S (2020) *Webcomics*, 1st ed., London: Bloomsbury Academic.

KOCCA Korea Creative Content Agency (n.d.) KOCCA. Retrieved 14 October 2022, from www.kocca.kr/en/main.do.

Korea Times (2021, December 24) Korean Webtoon Market Jumps to Top 1 Trillion Won in Sales in 2020. *Koreatimes*. www.koreatimes.co.kr/www/art/2022/08/398_321104.html.

Krecic (Mongie), LM (2022, August 29) Becoming a Webtoon Creator – Leeanne M. Krecic (MONGIE). www.mongrelmarie.com/becoming-a-webtoon-creator/.

Lamerichs, N (2020) Scrolling, Swiping, Selling: Understanding Webtoons and the Data-Driven Participatory Culture Around Comics. *Participations: Journal of Audience and Reception Studies*, 17(2), 211–229.

Lee, J, and In-Soo, S (2022) V&A · A brief history of webtoons. Retrieved 10 November 2022, from www.vam.ac.uk/articles/a-brief-history-of-webtoons.

Library of Congress (2014, present) Webcomics Web Archive. [Digital Collection]. Retrieved 24 May 2023, from www.loc.gov/collections/webcomics-web-archive/about-this-collection/.

Liu, A (2013) From Reading to Social Computing. In K. M. Price and R. Siemens, eds., *Literary Studies in the Digital Age*, New York: Modern Language Association of America. https://doi.org/10.1632/lsda.2013.2.

Lunning, F (2015, March 31) Women Who Changed Free Expression Special: 24 Nengumi – Comic Book Legal Defense Fund. https://cbldf.org/2015/03/women-who-changed-free-expression-special-24-nengumi/

MacDonald, H (2018, November 6) Head of Content Tom Akel out at Line Webtoon. www.comicsbeat.com/head-of-content-tom-akel-out-at-line-webtoon/.

MacDonald, H (2020a, January 17) Sales Charts: The Top 30 comics on Webtoon in 2019. www.comicsbeat.com/sales-charts-the-top-30-comics-on-webtoon-in-2019/.

MacDonald, H (2020b, March 23) Steve Geppi Announces Diamond is Ceasing the Distribution of New Weekly Product. www.comicsbeat.com/steve-geppi-announces-diamond-is-ceasing-the-distribution-of-new-weekly-product/.

MacDonald, H (2020c, September 16) You'll Never Guess What the Comics Industry Looked Like 28 Years Ago. www.comicsbeat.com/comics-in-1992-youll-never-guess-what-the-comics-industry-looked-like-28-years-ago/.

MacDonald, H (2021, March 25) Marvel and PRH Sign Exclusive Distribution Deal for Comics and Graphic Novels to Comics Shops. www.comicsbeat.com/marvel-and-prh-sign-exclusive-distribution-deal-for-comics-and-graphic-novels-to-comics-shops/.

MacDonald, H (2022a, June 13) Webtoon Ads Take Over New York City's Hippest Subway Station. www.comicsbeat.com/webtoon-ads-take-over-new-york-citys-hippest-subway-station/.

MacDonald, H (2022b, September 21) Distribution Shuffle: Geppi's Response, and PRH's Majority Share. www.comicsbeat.com/comics-distribution-chart-geppi-prhs-majority-share/.

Mag Uidhir, C (2012) Comics and Collective Authorship. In A. Meskin and R. T. Cook, eds., *The Art of Comics: A Philosophical Approach*, Chichester:

Wiley-Blackwell, 47–66. https://books.google.com/books? hl=en&lr=&id=KLzSI5V5-h8C&oi=fnd&pg=PA47&dq=%22McCloud, +from+an%22+%22by+Aaron+Meskin+and+Roy+T.%22+%22the+pri mary+object+of+interest,+readers+have+also+developed%22+%22of +Age,+recognize+and+value+well%E2%80%90constructed+narratives,% 22+&ots=B08NTgrUfF&sig=qiBgfsbzF23qbQppHSjsxReftSg.

Manouach, I (2019) Peanuts minus Schulz: Distributed Labor as a Compositional Practice. *The Comics Grid: Journal of Comics Scholarship*, 9(1). https://doi.org/10.16995/cg.139.

Manovich, L (2013) *Software Takes Command*, London: Bloomsbury. www .bloomsburycollections.com/book/software-takes-command.

Martin, C (2017) With, Against or Beyond Print? Digital Comics in Search of a Specific Status. *The Comics Grid: Journal of Comics Scholarship*, 7(13). https://doi.org/10.16995/cg.106.

Marvel Comics (n.d.) Women of Marvel | Marvel. Retrieved 21 November 2022, from www.marvel.com/women-of-marvel.

McCloud, S (1994) *Understanding Comics*, New York: HarperPerennial.

McCloud, S (2000) *Reinventing Comics: How Imagination and Technology Are Revolutionizing an Art Form*, New York: HarperCollins.

McCloud, S (2009, February) The 'Infinite Canvas'. Retrieved 15 November 2022, from https://scottmccloud.com/4-inventions/canvas/.

McCluskey, M (2021, August 9) Goodreads' Problem With Extortion Scams and Review Bombing. *Time*. https://time.com/6078993/good reads-review-bombing/.

McMillan, G (2020, June 5) DC Cuts Ties With Diamond Comic Distributors. www.hollywoodreporter.com/movies/movie-features/ dc-cuts-ties-diamond-comic-distribution-1297309/.

Merryweather Media (n.d.) Merryweather Media (@Merryweatherey) / Twitter. Retrieved 29 November 2022, from https://twitter.com/ Merryweatherey.

Misemer, L (2019a) A Historical Approach to Webcomics: Digital Authorship in the Early 2000s. *The Comics Grid: Journal of Comics Scholarship*, 9(1), 1–21. https://doi.org/10.16995/cg.162.

Misemer, L (2019b) Serial Critique: The Counterpublic of Wimmen's Comix. *Inks: The Journal of the Comics Studies Society*, 3(1), 6–26. https://doi.org/10.1353/ink.2019.0001.

Misemer, L (2021) Webcomics. In R. Fawaz, S. Streeby, and D. E. Whaley, eds., *Keywords for Comics Studies*, New York: New York University Press, 218–222.

Mundt, M (2022, September 8) Open Letter to Webtoon. *Twitter*, Tweet. https://twitter.com/lovebot_webtoon/status/1567958628501721088.

Mundt, M, and Keels, C (2022, September 8) Open Letter To Webtoon. https://docs.google.com/document/d/17quwfFX2LQP83yBDHnCv mCSLKGG5cVOWX5WRROuAXnc/mobilebasic.

Murray, S (2015) Charting the Digital Literary Sphere. *Contemporary Literature*, 56(2), 311–339. www.jstor.org/stable/24735010.

Murray, S (2021) Secret Agents: Algorithmic Culture, Goodreads and Datafication of the Contemporary Book World. *European Journal of Cultural Studies*, 24(4), 970–989. https://doi.org/10.1177/136754941 9886026.

Murray, S (2022) Varieties of Digital Literary Studies: Micro, Macro, Meso. *Digital Humanities Quarterly*, 16(2). http://digitalhumanities.org// dhq/vol/16/2/000616/000616.html.

Niebler, V (2020) 'YouTubers Unite': Collective Action by YouTube Content Creators. *Transfer: European Review of Labour and Research*, 26 (2), 223–227. https://doi.org/10.1177/1024258920920810.

Okeda, D (2019) Manga and the Law. In N. Rousmaniere and R. Matsuba, eds., *Manga*, London: Thames and Hudson and The British Museum, 272–275.

Orbaugh, S (2003) Creativity and Constraint in Amateur 'Manga' Production. *U.S.-Japan Women's Journal*, (25), 104–124. www.jstor.org/stable/42771905.

Orme, S (2016) Femininity and Fandom: The Dual-Stigmatisation of Female Comic Book Fans. *Journal of Graphic Novels and Comics*, 7(4), 403–416. https://doi.org/10.1080/21504857.2016.1219958.

Park, E-J (2020, May 28) Naver Restructures Its Webtoon Empire for Expansion. *Korea JoongAng Daily*. https://koreajoongangdaily.joins.com/2020/05/28/industry/Naver-webtoon-Webtoon-Entertainment/20200528185008671.html.

Pellitteri M, Bouissou J-M, Fratta GD, Martorella C and Suvilay B (2008) *Il drago e la saetta: modelli, strategie e identità dell'immaginario giapponese.* Tunué.

Pereira de Carvalho, A (2016) Reconfiguring the Power Structure of the Comic Book Field: Crowdfunding and the Use of Social Networks. In C. Brienza and P. Johnston, eds., *Cultures of Comics Work*, New York: Palgrave Macmillan US, 251–263.

Pianzola, F (2021) *Digital Social Reading: Works in Progress*, Cambridge: MIT Press. https://wip.mitpress.mit.edu/digital-social-reading.

Pianzola, F, Rebora, S, and Lauer, G (2020) Wattpad as a Resource for Literary Studies: Quantitative and Qualitative Examples of the Importance of Digital Social Reading and Readers' Comments in the Margins. *PLOS ONE*, 15(1), e0226708. https://doi.org/10.1371/journal.pone.0226708.

Pixels and Panels (n.d.) A Regimented Work Process is a Double-Edged Sword | *Lemon Soda & Coffee*'s Cecilia. [Mp3]. https://podcast.ausha.co/pixels-panels-a-show-about-webcomics/28-a-regimented-work-process-is-a-double-edged-swor-lemon-soda-coffee-s-cecilia.

Presser, A, Braviano, G, and Côrte-Real, E (2021) Webtoons. : A Parameter Guide for Developing Webcomics Focused on Small

Screen Reading. *Convergences – Journal of Research and Arts Education*, 14 (28), 67–78. https://doi.org/10.53681/c1514225187514391s.28.28.

Presser, AB (2019) Mobile Comics: Comics' Design Features Focusing on Small Screen Devices. *Convergências – Revista de Investigação e Ensino Das Artes*, *VOL XII (24)*, XII(24), 1–8. http://convergencias.esart.ipcb .pt/?p=article&id=355.

Priego, E, and Wilkins, P (2018) The Question Concerning Comics as Technology: Gestell and Grid. *The Comics Grid: Journal of Comics Scholarship*, 8(16), 16. https://doi.org/10.16995/cg.133.

Priego Ramirez, EF (2011) *The Comic Book in the Age of Digital Reproduction*, London: University College London. https://figshare.com/articles/ _The_Comic_Book_in_the_Age_of_Digital_Reproduction/754575.

Rageul, A (2018) On the Pleasure of Coding Interface Narratives. *The Comics Grid: Journal of Comics Scholarship*, 8(3). https://doi.org/ 10.16995/cg.107.

Ramdarshan Bold, M (2018) The Return of the Social Author: Negotiating Authority and Influence on Wattpad. *Convergence: The International Journal of Research into New Media Technologies*, 24(2), 117–136. https://doi.org/10.1177/1354856516654459.

Ray Murray, P, and Squires, C (2013) The Digital Publishing Communications Circuit. *Book 2.0*, 3(1), 3–23. https://doi.org/ 10.1386/btwo.3.1.3_1.

Rebora, S, and Pianzola, F (2018) A New Research Programme for Reading Research: Analysing Comments in the Margins on Wattpad. *DigitCult – Scientific Journal on Digital Cultures*, 3(2), 19–36. https://doi.org/ 10.4399/97888255181532.

Resha, A (2020) The Blue Age of Comic Books. *Inks: The Journal of the Comics Studies Society*, 4(1), 66–81. https://doi.org/10.1353/ ink.2020.0003.

Robbins, T (2013) *Pretty in Ink: North American Women Cartoonists 1896–2010*, Seattle: Fantagraphics Books.

Sabin, R (1993) *Adult Comics: An Introduction*, London: Routledge.

Salkowitz, R (2021, December 7) Webtoon's North American CEO Ken Kim on the Platform's Staggering Growth, Reach and Connections with the U.S. Comics Market. Retrieved 12 October 2022, from https://icv2 .com/articles/columns/view/49929/webtoons-north-american-ceo-ken-kim-platforms-staggering-growth-reach-connections-u-s-comics-market.

Sato, S (2013) *Manga Poverty by Shuho Sato – Ebook | Scribd* (D. Luffey, Trans.), Manga Reborn. www.scribd.com/book/195360050/Manga-Poverty.

Schenker, B (2021, March 8) Demo-Graphics: Comic Fandom on Facebook – US Edition. https://graphicpolicy.com/2021/03/08/demo-graphics-comic-fandom-facebook-us-edition-18-2/.

Scott, S (2013) Fangirls in Refrigerators: The Politics of (In)visibility in Comic Book Culture. *Transformative Works and Cultures*, 13. https://doi.org/10.3983/twc.2013.0460.

Šejić, S (2018, January 4) Sunstone – Top Cow. Retrieved 11 October 2022, from https://topcow.com/sunstone/.

Skains, RL (2010) The Shifting Author – Reader Dynamic: Online Novel Communities as a Bridge from Print to Digital Literature. *Convergence*, 16(1), 95–111. https://doi.org/10.1177/1354856509347713.

Skains, RL (2019) *Digital Authorship: Publishing in the Attention Economy*, Cambridge: Cambridge University Press. www.cambridge.org/core/elements/digital-authorship/C47B1D69263C882BFFC20DFD9F290F38.

St Clair, W (2004) *The Reading Nation in the Romantic Period*, Cambridge: Cambridge University Press.

Stefanelli, M (2021, November 8) Le nuove major del fumetto saranno le aziende coreane di webtoon? Retrieved 17 May 2023, from https://fumettologica.it/2021/11/webtoon-fumetti-coreani/.

Tanski, K (2022a, March 4) The Symposium on Comic Arts: At the Intersections of Comics Education and Industry. https://womenwriteaboutcomics.com/2022/03/the-symposium-on-comic-arts-at-the-intersections-of-comics-education-and-industry/.

Tanski, K (2022b, September 19) Previously on Comics: Webtoon Drama Highlights Pay Disparity for Creators. https://womenwriteaboutcomics.com/2022/09/previously-on-comics-webtoon-drama-highlights-pay-disparity-for-creators/.

Taylor, H (2019) *Why Women Read Fiction: The Stories of Our Lives*, Oxford: Oxford University Press.

Thomas, A, Battisti, M, and Kretschmer, M (2022) *UK Authors' Earnings and Contracts: A Survey of 60.000 Writers*, Glasgow: UK Copyright and Creative Economy Research Centre (CREATe). https://zenodo.org/record/7373314.

WEBTOON (2021, November 5) Upcoming Update to Our Comment Moderation System. Retrieved 21 November 2022, from www.webtoons.com/en/notice/detail?noticeNo=2246.

WEBTOON (2022a, March 14) Community Policy | WEBTOON. Retrieved 27 June 2022, from www.webtoons.com/en/terms/canvasPolicy.

WEBTOON (2022b, June 2) 2022 Call to Action Contest Frequently Asked Questions. Retrieved 29 June 2022, from www.webtoons.com/en/notice/detail?noticeNo=2572.

WEBTOON (2023a) WEBTOON Fact Sheet – 2023 .pdf.

WEBTOON (2023b, June 27) Terms of Use | WEBTOON. Retrieved 28 June 2023, from www.webtoons.com/en/terms.

WEBTOON (n.d.-a) WEBTOON – The Official Home for All Things WEBTOON. Retrieved 29 November 2022, from www.webtoons.com/en/dailySchedule.

WEBTOON (n.d.-b) Webtoon Canvas: The Next Great Webcomic Is Here. Retrieved 14 October 2022, from www.webtoons.com/en/challenge.

Woo, B (2018) Is There a Comic Book Industry? *Media Industries Journal*, 5 (1), 27–46. https://doi.org/10.3998/mij.15031809.0005.102.

Woo, B (2021) The Comics Workforce. In B. Woo and J. Stoll, eds., *The Comics World: Comic Books, Graphic Novels, and Their Publics*, Jackson, MS: University Press of Mississippi, 6–18.

Yasuda, K, and Satomi, N (2019) Interview: Yasuda Kahoru and Satomi Naoki, Comiket Organisers. In N. Rousmaniere and R. Matsuba, eds., *Manga*, London: Thames and Hudson and The British Museum, 268–271.

Yecies, B, and Shim, A-G (2021) *South Korea's Webtooniverse and the Digital Comic Revolution*, Lanham: Rowman & Littlefield.

Yim, S-H (2022, July 27) Webtoon Version of 'Extraordinary Attorney Woo' to be Released Tonight on Naver Webtoon. *Korea JoongAng Daily*. https://koreajoongangdaily.joins.com/2022/07/27/culture/gamesWebtoons/webtoon-extraordinary-attorney-woo-naver-webtoon/20220727133717164.html.

Yoon, S-Y (2021, October 2) Kakao Forced to Reexamine How It Treats Webtoon Artists. https://koreajoongangdaily.joins.com/2021/10/02/business/tech/Kakao-Entertainment-Naver-Webtoon-webtoon/20211002070002822.html.

Yoon, S-Y (2022a, April 2) [WHY] The Rise of Webtoons Means Fat Pay Checks, but Only for a Few. *Korea JoongAng Daily*. https://koreajoongangdaily.joins.com/2022/04/02/business/industry/webtoon-webtoonist-Naver/20220402070019357.html.

Yoon, S-Y (2022b, August 25) Kakao to Spend 10 Billion Won Funding Authors and Artists. *Korea JoongAng Daily*. https://koreajoongangda ily.joins.com/2022/08/25/business/industry/Korea-webtoon-web-novel/20220825175243729.html.

Zhdanova, M (2021, November 12) A Brief History of Webcomics: 2010 to Now. https://womenwriteaboutcomics.com/2021/11/history-webco mics-now/.

Acknowledgements

This Element would not have been possible without the support of several colleagues who provided feedback, advice and encouragement at numerous key moments during its composition.

First, I wish to thank my past and present Open University colleagues in the Digital Humanities and History of Books and Reading research collaborations: Alessio Antonini, Sally Blackburn-Daniels, David King, Edmund King and Shafquat Towheed. This study would not have been possible without your support and the many conversations where you shared your wisdom, expertise and insight. The READ-IT project provided the first occasion for the airing of my research plans, followed by the Gender and Otherness in the Humanities (GOTH) seminars at The Open University and by the University of East Anglia's Data Drop-Ins. A thank you to all colleagues there for your questions, comments, and curiosity, which led me to refine the ideas behind this work. My gratitude also to Linda Berube and Ernesto Priego, co-organisers with me of the Web/Comics Workshop at the 2023 Hypertext conference, where this book coalesced and took shape.

I am grateful to my research and career mentors Phil Perkins and Nicola Watson, who encouraged me to write, and to persist when times were rough. Special thanks to The Open University Library's Nicola Dowson and Guy Lavender and to my editors Laura Dietz and Samantha Rayner for their advice on the challenging issues this Element had to overcome. Your unwavering support and guidance enabled me to persevere and reach a solution. Thanks also to the peer reviewers for their comments and advice, which have made this element clearer and stronger. In addition, I wish to acknowledge the support I have received from the Faculty of Arts and Social Sciences in the form of a grant from the Strategic Research Investment Fund, which has enabled the open access publication of this Element.

My final thanks are to my family, who endured months of discussion (and obsession) about webtoons and webcomics, and to my counsellor, Carole, who persuaded me to undertake this project. I promised I would dedicate my book to you, and here it is.

Cambridge Elements ≡

Publishing and Book Culture

SERIES EDITOR
Samantha Rayner
University College London

Samantha Rayner is Professor of Publishing and Book Cultures
at UCL. She is also Director of UCL's Centre for Publishing,
co-Director of the Bloomsbury CHAPTER (Communication
History, Authorship, Publishing, Textual Editing and
Reading) and co-Chair of the Bookselling Research Network.

ASSOCIATE EDITOR
Leah Tether
University of Bristol

Leah Tether is Professor of Medieval Literature and Publishing
at the University of Bristol. With an academic background in
medieval French and English literature and a professional
background in trade publishing, Leah has combined her
expertise and developed an international research profile in
book and publishing history from manuscript to digital.

ABOUT THE SERIES

This series aims to fill the demand for easily accessible, quality texts available for teaching and research in the diverse and dynamic fields of Publishing and Book Culture. Rigorously researched and peer-reviewed Elements will be published under themes, or 'Gatherings'. These Elements should be the first check point for researchers or students working on that area of publishing and book trade history and practice: we hope that, situated so logically at Cambridge University Press, where academic publishing in the UK began, it will develop to create an unrivalled space where these histories and practices can be investigated and preserved.

Cambridge Elements ☰

Publishing and Book Culture

DIGITAL LITERARY CULTURE
Gathering Editor: Laura Dietz
Laura Dietz is Associate Professor of Writing and Digital
Publishing Studies in the Cambridge School of Creative
Industries at Anglia Ruskin University. She writes novels and
studies novels, publishing fiction alongside research on topics such
as e-novel readership, the digital short story, online literary
magazines, and the changing definition of authorship
in the digital era.

ELEMENTS IN THE GATHERING

A full series listing is available at: www.cambridge.org/EPBC

Milton Keynes UK
Ingram Content Group UK Ltd.
UKHW022025290924
448880UK00016B/58